The Ghost on the Ramparts

Books by Robert B. Heilman

America in English Fiction 1760-1800 (1937)
This Great Stage: Image and Structure in King Lear (1948)
Magic in the Web: Action and Language in Othello (1956)
Tragedy and Melodrama: Versions of Experience (1968)
The Iceman, the Arsonist, and the Troubled Agent: Tragedy and Melodrama on the Modern Stage (1973)
The Ghost on the Ramparts and Other Essays in the Humanities (1973)

THE GHOST ON THE RAMPARTS
AND OTHER ESSAYS
IN THE HUMANITIES

ROBERT B. HEILMAN

University of Georgia Press · Athens

Library of Congress Catalog Card Number: 72-86782
International Standard Book Number: 0-8203-0297-x

The University of Georgia Press, Athens 30601
Copyright 1973 by the University of Georgia Press

Printed in the United States of America

To Dorothee N. Bowie and Andrew R. Hilen
and to the memory of James W. Hall

Contents

IN THE STUDY
HISTORICAL AND CRITICAL APPROACHES

AT THE BOTTOM OF EVERYTHING
HUMANITIES

Preface

First, a word about the title. It was of course convenient to borrow the caption of the first essay and use it as the title of the book. But in this there was a whisper of profits as well as convenience. Invariably anything Hamletic intimates a large world and major problems, and who could question the rightness of this suggestion for the humanities, in academe or outside? But still, modesty along with magnitude: not the young hero facing an unprecedented moral crisis alone, but instead an older member of the family, a retired administrator making only brief walk-on appearances in an advisory role. Granted, he makes rather a point of his being on "the ramparts," perhaps the high positions that he thinks to defend, but perhaps no more than the platforms where speakers characteristically hold forth after sundown. He may have at times an air of knowing more than he can tell, and yet of not being sure that he is getting through. As a ghost he may be claiming spiritual powers or acknowledging grave limitations; he may seem, on the one hand, faded and insubstantial, or, on the other, lugubrious and menacing. He can hardly help being a little admonitory, calling a name or two, persisting a bit vehemently. But he does carefully observe time limits. Insofar as he laments, he laments not crimes but follies—mistakes, misconceptions, misadventures, misalliances; and necessarily he points to the deeds of good sense without which we could not identify follies. His ear trouble is not at all personal, but representative: innumerable ears have had to receive the strange potions concocted and decanted by aspirants to new marriages, old thrones, and revised mores in the educational realm.

 The Ghost on the Ramparts comprises essays on education that have seemed worth bringing together in one volume. "Education" means, for the most part, what goes on in departments of English, though the subject is at times the humanities generally, and occasionally the new pedagogical inventions that spring up and spread around like wild morning glory without regard for fenced fields. When the subject is clearly departments of English, the departments are principally those of colleges and universities. Several pieces, however, were meant for a special audience of honor students ("Freedom from Speech") or for audiences of high-school and junior-college teachers ("Literature and Growing Up," "Teaching Careers and Graduate Schools") and doubt-less retain evidences of their origin, though in revising them I have meant to make them as widely meaningful and applicable as possible. Some of the essays came out of my own desire to explore an issue; some were responses to requests by editors; some were invited "talks," "lectures," or "addresses." "The Cult of Personality" was the "presi-dential address" at an annual meeting of the Philological Association of the Pacific Coast; "Humanisticism and Melodrama" was a "dinner address" at an annual meeting of the Rocky Mountain Modern Lan-guage Association; and "Clichés and Anticlichés" was the same for the South Central Modern Language Association. "Verbal Traffic and Moral Freight" was the Father William Costello Memorial Lec-ture at Gonzaga University. "Historian and Critic" was a "talk" at the American Embassy in London and a "lecture" at several English and German universities. But it is a truism of bookmaking that words adjusted to the ears of a physically present audience are likely to dis-tress the eyes of a reader; hence, as far as possible, the symptoms of a style for public hearing have yielded to the habits of prose for private reading. However, I have let stand some of the remarks to the audi-ence in "The Ghost on the Ramparts," a "keynote address" to an institute for incoming department chairmen, and in "Except He Come to Composition," a "talk" to the Conference on College Composition and Communication at its annual meeting, since in both of these what is said grows partly out of an interplay between a particular personal experience and a particular audience—an interplay, however, which I hope will invite eavesdropping by those who do not belong to either of the groups.

The final diversity among these essays is that they were written during three decades—three in the 1950s, seven in the 1960s, and four in the 1970s. Thus they have taken form in enough different historical contexts to make them, insofar as they are topical, reflect more than one set of topical issues. On the other hand more than half of them come after 1965, and an even half in the last five years; thus they may be supposed to have as much bearing as they should on recent educational combats. In revising them, I have wanted, for tactical ends, to have the essays somewhat attuned to the movements by which the fairly stable underlying educational activity acquires different façades from one decade to another. By this I do not mean simple updating, redecorating the obsolete, or getting with current events. If one is trying to put a finger on the durable aspects of education, the goals and methods that remain constant, one is not recycling the outworn by interpolating topical allusions. If one is speaking of what is achieved by the reading of literature, or by precision in language, or by understanding how the humanities function vis-à-vis the world, one is not reporting on some past or passing fashion or on some unstable compound that alters essentially with every change of the influencing atmosphere. With such themes contemporary relevance is an irrelevance. But in dealing with what one believes to be the nondating, one may present it the better, perhaps, by utilizing the perspectives which alter each year as various prophets descend from the mountains or ascend from the abysses and let us share in the epiphanies which they have experienced above or below. If one is making a case for the reading of literature, his central theme does not change; but his way into the theme, and his emphases, will vary if he conceives of "the enemy" as basic illiteracy, muddled values, or electronic distractions. If one is making a case for hard and well-creased precision of speech (that it should have to be made!), he can clarify the better by calling attention to the thought-preventing clichés and slogans of the day; in the 1970s, presumably, one could make less headway against the hackneyed and the propagandistic by alluding to "the cross of gold" or "the big stick" or "the war to end war" than one could by alluding to "the system" or "the corruption of the over-30s." Or if one is arguing that a grading system is a useful part of the educational enterprise, he will proceed differently if the problem is the compulsory egalitarianism of the "credit/no credit" dogma or the elective egalitarianism of the "gentleman's C" (that once goal of amiable adversaries whom it was delightful to betray, when one could, into the apostasy of a B or A). In revising, then, I have wanted to extend to later developments a minimal awareness without which certain topics might accidentally seem to have less than their true and enduring aliveness (since headlines, alas, are often the sole criteria of aliveness).

Even in essays separated by some years there is an obvious continuity of thought or at least of attitude. This is evidenced by the reappearance of certain topics in different contexts. I have tried to eliminate passages in which I seemed only to be borrowing from myself, but I have let stand repetitions which I thought would contribute to emphasis rather than ennui. Hence there appear, more than once, "gut reaction," "doing one's thing," the misconceptions of change and relevance and of the importance of student and faculty "interests," the problem of "growing up," the uses of "vicarious experience," the tendency of even intellectuals to fall into good guys versus bad guys interpretations, the problem of some faulty ideas of faculty freedom and prerogative, of the sense of "my course" and of "what I want to do."

The continuity of point of view makes possible an inner form without which such a collection would be a mechanical assemblage rather than the book I hope it is. In one sense the point of view is that of a professional man with certain persisting convictions; in another it is that of a perennial chairman who wrote all parts of the book during his chairmanship. As I observe in the first essay, there are reasons why a chairman has a particularly good vantage point for surveying the profession. But at the same time he should be aware of the biases that his job makes him liable to—chiefly, I suppose, the sense that order, even in an imperfect and errant form, is less like oppression than revolution is like oppression-begetting chaos. If he can allow for this, he may find the independence and balance and, if he is lucky enough, the soundness that will be evidenced by the displeasure of both extreme right and extreme left.

The essays appear to fall naturally into an arrangement that gives the book a meaningful structure. It is logical, I believe, for an ex-chairman to begin with his sense of how a chairmanship operates. It is natural for him then to go on and talk about the values that an English department is supposed to serve. He may be expected to have some views on what can be accomplished by the reading of literature, by the experience of composition if it is rightly understood as a discipline (chapters 2–4). And, to continue with what goes on in the classroom, he is pretty likely to have a concept of pedagogical style—of the kind of posture that faculty members have toward students, toward courses, toward degrees, toward the raw materials out of which books and courses are made, toward themselves (chapters 5 and 6). Since pedagogical style is in part a matter of verbal style, and since reading leads to both writing and discussion, the observer of the profession can hardly help saying something about good writing and rational discourse, and in particular about the kinds of vocabulary that prevent fuzziness, nonthought, the deception of self and others, self-inflation, and the self-congratulation implicit in verbal fashionableness (chapters 7–9). He would be exceptional if he did not have some convictions about the two intellectual instruments that have battled in his field since about 1930, history and criticism. I, for one, find interest in the conflicting American tendencies to discard history and to enthrone it, and in the kinds of intellectual personality that pursue literature in terms of its external and its internal relations (chapters 10 and 11). The final section tries to get to certain underlying issues that we cannot take for granted—the characteristics which distinguish humanistic study from science, preserve it against excessive simplicities, and separate it wholly from the politics that, from one extreme or the other, always wants education to be its slave (chapters 12–14).

Sometimes the commentator describes, sometimes he exhorts, sometimes he theorizes. Theory is the main business of the last five essays. I have given the emphatic final position to "Humanistic Education as Comedy." There are several reasons for this. For one thing, the title suggests that our professional business, though serious indeed, is not solemn, and that at times the way we carry it on may be laughable. For another the essay tries to expound humanistic education by using a totally new perspective, to get to the essence by the strange route of literary analogy. Finally the method discovers in the essence of humanistic education a resistance to two lamentable counter-extremes—the one that wants education only to serve a present unchanging world, and the one that wants it to become only a tool of those committed to total change.

I am grateful to various organizations and editors for providing me with opportunities to air my views on different aspects of what we do in the field of English. Though acknowledgment of permission to reprint is made elsewhere, I want especially to mention several editors—William Irmscher, Andrew Lytle, and Lewis Simpson—whose granting of permission continues pleasant relationships that have been of long standing. Sherry Laing was of great help in preparing the manuscript. My wife has continued unflinching in the old role of test audience for these verbal flights, and has had a sharp ear for both stuttering engines and sonic booms.

In dedicating the volume to Mrs. Dorothee N. Bowie, Andrew R. Hilen, and the memory of James W. Hall I want to acknowledge their friendship, their talent in the administration which for some years was our joint task, and their shrewd knowledge of the profession. Dorothee Bowie, the professional administrator, made it possible for the rest of us to write; Andrew Hilen and James Hall, as faculty administrators should be, were first of all excellent teachers and scholars. James Hall's sudden death in 1971 was a sad loss to students and to colleagues both in our department and in the field of modern literature, in which he was an unusually perceptive critic.

ROBERT B. HEILMAN

London, May 1972

IN THE FRONT OFFICE

I
The Ghost
on the Ramparts

A Chairman on the Chairmanship

We chairmen now settle down to chores. We have wined and dined and we need a little penance to be sure we aren't only playing. An educational week should have a somewhat mournful tone lest it seem not educational. I am the transition from Mardi Gras's fires (though it's only a fat Monday) to Wednesday's ashes, the summons from living too well back to a better life, the guide from carnival forgetting to a long Lent of learning. The scheduled speaker is surefire mortification; whatever his style he can inflict the discomforts that seem to guarantee salvation. If he jests, he will seem light-minded; if he moralizes, he will seem heavy-handed; if he lets his fellows off the hook too soon, he will seem to shortchange them; if he is thorough, he will seem long-winded. He is the natural bridge of sighs from Monday martinis to midweek martyrdom.

The program calls this sobering homily the keynote address. After I had said I would do it, I found I did not know what it is. I had only a vague image of the Chicago where I was to hold forth—an image of warmish weather, tumultuous delegates, indoor marching mobs, futile gavels, a weedpatch of microphones, an orator whom no one had ever heard of but who got two minutes of cheering after every period and sometimes after the commas. This seemed too good to be true, so like the freshman in search of a theme, I tried the dictionaries. One says the keynoter "presents the essential issues of interest to the assembly." Pretty tame, that. I tried another. It says the keynote is "the line of policy . . . as set forth authoritatively in advance in a public speech." I like that. Authoritatively—that adverb so rare in the chairman's life!

Yet the authority comes only from the acquiescence of the listeners. So it is only spiritual, or, in older idiom, ghostly. This is fitting in another sense. For I am one of the old-time chairmen who would get into office and just stay on forever—not one of those newfangled types whose headships are cut off by triennial or quinquennial legal guillotines. I speak, as it were, from a former age, and I feel a bit like the wraith of Hamlet senior—perhaps a truepenny, perhaps an old mole in the cellarage, crying to his juniors, "Swear!"; an apparition who could a tale unfold, who might tempt men toward the flood or the dreadful summit of the cliff, but who might reveal the treasure uphoarded in his life, who might be privy to his country's fate and tell what foreknowing may avoid. But playing ghost runs the risk of retort from young Danes. Some kindly courtier here might urge, "Stay, illusion. . . . Speak to me." But another might complain of one who usurps this time of night; a crueler one might simply imitate the cock's crow. Then it would be small satisfaction for the ghost to stalk away, offended, or even to recall that he is, as the air, invulnerable.

A new chairman is usually tapped as heir to a time that is out of joint, and drafted to be its orthopedic surgeon. He tends quickly to fall into the habit of soliloquy. Hence the keynote address might aspire to be the monologue that will end soliloquies. No keynoter can do it, alas. He can only cry: pity me not, but lend thine serious hearing to what I shall unfold.

Before the cock crows, I hope to toss off a few do's and don't's of palace management. My problem is that last year John Gerber outlined administrative desiderata with great concreteness, fullness, and perceptiveness. I might argue with him, and cast my brains in doubt; plagiarize him, and cast my morals in doubt; or try to be different, and cast my taste in doubt. Almost by chance I settle on the third risk. I shall try a slightly more abstract theme, look a little more at the inner landscape. I shall glance at certain attitudes by which the chairman may define his role—such as his attitudes to himself, his post, his superiors, his colleagues. Here I can toss together observation, theory, indecisive meditation, cocksure obiter dicta, recollection, guesses, and tips. It is a mixed grill. Somewhere in it I hope there is some meat.

The chairman needs first of all to have an adequate working attitude to himself as an academic man called to a chairmanship. He should never think of himself as a lost scholar or critic or teacher who, by popular demand and despite his own screams of horror, was from his alma mater's class-womb untimely ripped and set forcibly upon the throne. If he does not think of himself this way, he will not talk of himself this way, and thus he will spare auditors the embarrassment of listening to what they will rightly think of as fishy. He should never feel sorry for himself; all he has to do is get out, according to Truman's Law. Nor can he precisely say he sought and loves the chairmanship, for this runs counter to the academic superstition—academe has more superstitions than Wessex—that the only good administrators are those who, like a caveman's girlfriend, are clubbed into the work. He is not obligated by integrity to offend the superstitions that make proudly rational men happy. But there is a middle ground between phony unwillingness and redundant eagerness—one that introduces no clichés, self-pity, soothing syrup, or false modesty: he can think that he is in the job, and say that he is, simply because the job, or some aspects of it, correspond to certain elements in himself. Privately he can live with the fact that the elements may be noble, less noble, ignoble, neutral, or a mixture; and he can let others make up their own minds which of these dominates (they will not shirk this duty). It is, I think, a respectable way of accounting for the fact that jobs and suitable occupants do tend to come together, without an unseemly forcing of the unwilling man, or an unseemly pursuit by an overwilling man.

Once he has a bearable understanding of himself in his post, the chairman needs a usable attitude to the working of the post and to his working in it. Let him avoid clichés about accepting challenges and conducting dialogues. Let him not think of himself basically as a servitor, a factotum, a legman, a you-name-it-I'll-get-it-done type, a yes-man for his precinct. No first-rate man, no potentially first-rate administrator will or can think of himself as one who simply translates the will of others into deeds. Privately, of course, he must be willing to accept such roles. He must do chores, execute group decisions. Hence he should not, at the other extreme, think of himself as essentially a big policy man, an idea man, an outsize mind who can leave details, routines, housekeeping, and KP duties to others. As a matter of fact a good deal of policy is made by the very handling of routine and detail—by the selection of committees, the working out of teaching schedules, the management of those lesser parts of the budget where there is a little room for choice. The chairman's way of handling routine replies to hundreds of letters of application, or the routines of an interview gone through for the fiftieth time, may do more than the noblest generalizations to create in applicants a sense of his school and to get acceptances from them. In sum the chairman should not act either like a little man waiting to be told what to do, or like a big man who only makes big decisions and thus tells others what to do. Let him be prepared for drudgery, and at the same time find, in the machinery amid which he inevitably lives, the devices by which gradually to move affairs in a desirable direction. Thus his colleagues may now and then realize, without too much pain of contentious confron-

5

tation, that they have discovered a new way of doing things.

The chairman should not think of his post as one without power, for he can quietly find ways to exercise it. There is too much sentimentality about power, as if it were inherently evil and no good man could enjoy it. It is inherently neutral, virtually all men enjoy it, and the chairman should relish using it for ends that he believes in. Sometimes he can use it to adjust inequities that result from drift, accident, indifference, or the way a committee or department vote has gone. Most regularly he can use it to move rewards in the right direction. Of the satisfactions possible to the chairman, I know none greater than that of having steered due perquisites to persons who contribute most to the well-being of the institution (they are, by the way, not always people that he loves). Obviously the relish of power has to be balanced by the knowledge that power corrupts, and perhaps his never-ending vigilance against being corrupted is one of the subtler excitements of the chairman's role. He is never sure, of course, for he can deceive himself. The natural panacea for his self-deception is the vigilance of colleagues; in this regard he can count on their moral energy (if not always their perspicacity, since the chairmanship is likely to mislead others besides its occupant). But the chairman has a still sounder way of monitoring himself in the exercise of power: he can perform every act, make every decision, as if it were going to be audited, or even scrutinized by an investigating committee. I recommend this attitude of mind, for the sense of a possible public audit is a remarkable protection against any actions, however tempting, that would look sickly under scrutiny. Yet in rare cases the chairman has to forget this simulated doomsday and gamble on his intuition, that is, rely on evidence not yet in being, or on quality not yet evidenced. Then he will have to brazen his way through whatever audit there is, and only hope that the ultimate sterner inspection, the audit by history, will not prove him a fool or a sentimentalist or a misguided partisan.

Next, the chairman has to live in a very uncertain area where he must manage two complementary attitudes—the one to the administration, and the other to his department faculty. Here he must boldly imagine himself to be Ulysses, watchful at once against Scylla, the monster high up on the cliff, and Charybdis, the whirlpool below. The administration will think him a disturber of their peace and an insatiable agent of a malcontent faculty; the latter will think him a policeman to them and a stooge to dean and president. The administration want him to be a fire chief, and the faculty want him to be the chief incendiary. If he antagonizes either side unbearably, the chairman cannot survive, and since part of his business is to survive, he may seem to acquire a Ulyssean duplicity. But despite pressures from above

6

and from around, he has a rather wide range of honorable choices. For one thing the administration won't fire him unless he is truly outrageous, for getting rid of him means finding a replacement in a day when there are more vacancies than glamorous applicants. The faculty are strongly attracted to regicide, but they tend to stop short just at the chopping block, suddenly alarmed by the horrid fact that to bear the ills they have may be a lesser evil than flying to others that they know not of. One option open to the chairman is to play administration and department against each other: to tell either side that the other won't stand for it, whether the *it* is an ill-advised ruling from above or a snatch at oversized privilege from below. At times this *is* an appropriate tactic, but it is an inadequate model because it implies that quick footwork, sleight of hand, and poker finesse will always do. They won't. Nor can the chairman have a permanent partisan stance; by it he would be immobilized. On the other hand he can't mechanically play it now one way and now the other; this makes him too mobile, and neither side will trust him. In the end he can't avoid making one judgment after another as one pressure after another comes up; what he has to do, every time, is decide who is operating with the better sense of institutional well-being. If the administration resists a promotion that has been voted on sentimental grounds, the chairman has to be unreservedly proadministration, for one sentimental promotion begets another, and the habit of voting feeling instead of the record is a sure route to department mediocrity. (This assumes that the chairman can spot a sentimental promotion; if he can't, he should be, not a chairman, but an ombudsman.) If the administration wants the chairman to try to damp down a colleague who suffers from the omniscience syndrome and is therefore making stunning public pronouncements on every subject but literature, the chairman has to be profaculty (though he may get together with the dean and drink to laryngitis for his colleague). Obviously, living with a tasteless prophet is a lesser evil, institutionally, than letting the impression get around that there is an official code for the regulation of local prophets.

The new chairman, fresh out of the faculty, may still be in the shadow of the faculty sense of infallibility. So I should warn him not to be surprised, or to suspect himself of apostasy, if he finds the administration making a better record than he anticipated. In our day it is often the administrator who has the more thoroughgoing commitment to the institution. The institutional quality is his teacher's rating, his bibliography, his toehold on immortality, and he may do very well by it indeed. Granted, he may err from defective talent or defective imagination, or the very human tendency to consider his own wishes the best source of institutional health (the same sources of error, by the way, that we see in the faculty). But his commitment is conspicuous precisely because, in our day, faculty commitment is not conspicuous. The usual cliché is that the faculty's loyalty is not to the institution but to the profession. Too often, unfortunately, the loyalty is not even to the profession but simply to the professor himself, and such a loyalist tends to regard improvement in the institution as an automatic by-product of privileges for himself. If the administrator would like us to think that in his will is our peace, the offer-crowned professor is likely to think that in his bill is our piece of institutional good luck.

The chairman needs to consider his attitude to the kind of movement his department should have. He may well find that his best role is that of counterbalance or counterweight. He ought to seek a middle ground between whoring after novelty and regularly celebrating golden anniversaries of being married to the same old thing. If, in terms of its interests, methods, and emphasis, his department is on the monogamous side, he ought to parade some new fancy ladies before it and hope that some sparks will be struck. But perhaps his department already suffers from the wandering eye, drifting from one beauty queen to another, and getting successive crushes on Miss Semantics, Miss Linguistics, Miss Teacher Training, Miss ABD Degree, Miss Pass-Fail, Miss No Grades, Miss No Requirements, Miss No Composition, Miss Independent Study, Miss Fickle Curriculum (engaged every year to a different innovative seducer), and other such 36–22–36 types. He may then feel obligated to resist promiscuity. Needless to say, I do not propose to ignore or pretend to dispose of such seductive new developments, but we ought to realize that we live in an era not only of change, but dedicated to change, mad about change, and quite naive about change, so that all change seems good change, and all motion forward motion. Hence a new chairman is quite likely to think that change is his obligation, and that all innovation is salvation. In his particular department it may be, but that is to be decided in each case. In general, change is not obligatory; what is chic may be neither useful nor healthful; and all fads and fashions need a cool eye—even when they are apparently endorsed by national organizations. Several years ago some assembler of statistics discovered that many teachers of high-school English had had no course in advanced composition, and so there went up a great hue and cry about making teacher-training curricula include a course in advanced composition—three magic hours. As far as I know, the central question was unexamined and was totally begged—namely, the efficacy of a course in advanced composition in improving the teaching of high-school English. It is hard to examine a landslide while it is sliding, or to accuse a roaring avalanche

8

of begging questions, but the chairman ought occasionally to risk it.

Or, to shift images, the chairman who gets his hand in the hole in the dike soon enough may prevent a flood. By the dike I mean all that protects a rational and nurturing use of the humanities against emotional torrents pretending to be the bearers of new life. Several of these are now making small holes in the dike. One is that the study of literature is a form of psychotherapy—a new form of an old leak that first threatened when Miss Communications was alluring pedagogical hearts ripe for an affair with a new charmer. The next is that we should be teaching the person and not the subject—a sort of secular jesuitry in which the instructor plays at directing consciousness. Another is that literary study should be a stimulation and communion of souls (the magic circle of feelings at play) rather than an informing of minds and a disciplining of imaginations. Or, in slightly different terms, the study of literature should be an experience rather than a critique of experience: hence the passion for audio-visual accompaniments, tapes, records, slides, cinemas, and all the devices of nonmind that tend to substitute a simplistic participation for the complex analytical role which involves both imaginative identification and critical detachment. The chairman should not be surprised if some of his staff want him to budget light shows to get the class into the mood of *Lear* or *The Ancient Mariner* or *Wuthering Heights* or *The Turn of the Screw*.

But of all these small currents that want to burst out and flood the land, the one that in a way speaks for all the others and is closest to wrecking the dike is the cry for relevance. It is one of the main question-begging cant words of our day; threatening because undefined, it terrifies some schoolmen into crying *peccavi*'s like defendants at a Stalinist treason trial, as if they had continually, genocidally practiced wilful, first-degree irrelevance. (While self-correction is seemly, modish, uncritical self-castigation is not.) Some of the moral energy of all of us—but especially of chairmen—should go into asking what the evangelists of relevance mean, and what they want. Our documents are inevitably topical in past contexts; do the releventrepreneurs want us to make even our monuments topical, and in passing contexts? To make Chaucer speak on Vietnam? Browning on geriatrics ("the best is yet to be")? Dickens on guaranteed national income? Or shall we read only twentieth-century American literature? Or concentrate on black writers? I hope this is a parody, but I am not at all sure that it is.

Relevance can, however, be understood in a way compatible with the nature of literature in itself and as the materials of instruction. What literature is relevant to, what it must be taught as relevant to, is an inclusive human reality, the reality both of human nature and of the human situation, which persists despite the constricting and deforming

9

tendencies which help give every age its recognizable character. In this relevance it helps maintain the age's awareness of a larger human truth than the age itself, with its defining biases and antagonisms and self-assured novelties, can ever accommodate. We live in a particular kind of narrow age—one that is strong on the hidden motive, the variants of sex, the iddish underside, malice, and destructiveness, but quite weak on other aspects of personality. Without the sense of the whole truth that literature can give (and that religion can give, except that it is misunderstood by even more people than misconceive literature) we of this age are quite likely to kill each other all off because we honestly think that that is all we can do.

What is particularly relevant to our needs, then, is the kind of sensibility we find in George Eliot, with her almost unlimited sense of human potential. Take *Middlemarch*. At its center we find not only a profound sense of human fallibility and lacerating egotism, but a conviction that a foolish idealism can finally set foot on solid ground without losing either a sense of the good to be pursued or the energy to pursue it; that an emotionally injured person can surmount the sense of injury and act generously; and that generous action can excite unselfish conduct in the most self-centered of beings. In these matters is the heart of relevance for an age that would have great difficulty in making such assertions; their relevance is that they might bring our partial beings a little closer to wholeness. This is not the easy nickel-in-the-slot relevance.

I go into so much detail only in the hope of making concrete the issue of the chairman's attitude to change, that is, to all the panaceas that come rolling down the pike promising to pop us into an instant brave new world. Some of them he will approve; others he may have to buy because so many colleagues, burdened with our characteristic recent fear of being in a rut, believe in them. But the chairman can try to be selective; he can call for a definition of terms; he can escape the illusion that to be different from what one was is surely to be better; and he can keep ever alert his eschatological sense—his awareness of the final things toward which each innovation leads. He should remember that while "make it new" may be a valid injunction for an artist, the comparable rule for the teacher is "make it true." It is a harder prescription.

Finally the chairman must discover a manageable attitude to the human beings on his staff. He is better off if he is more curious than censorious, if he can be surprised without being outraged, and if he can be unillusioned without being disillusioned. As chairman he is more exposed than anyone else to the self-seeking side of his colleagues, to the unsteady sense of reality, to the longing for privilege, to the lingeringly immature, to the envious, the complacent, the cantankerous, the niggling, the undependable, the disruptive. They will complain about offices, office equipment, teaching schedules, parking arrangements, classroom assignments, secretarial procedures, the distance to lavatories; to gain extra services or goods (to which they are often not entitled), they will wheedle, grieve, bluff, and even be devious. Some are at odds with group decisions—say on course contents or textbooks—and there is even a recent tendency to resist these on grounds of personal freedom. Here we get into that area of principles and causes in which the chairman will find some fairly complex behavior. Occasionally he will run into an honest, forthright, passionate colleague from whom he will do well to learn: the man's profound concern for an issue—say black education or Ph.D. requirements—may stimulate the chairman to a sharper awareness than he has had. He needs stimuli of this kind. But he will also observe that when cause and principle get into the picture, motives other than love of justice are often at work. Causes always attract plotters; some men just plot spontaneously, but most lovers of plotting need façades of virtue. A cause justifies keeping things stirred up, arousing oppositions. Some people do this just for kicks. Others seek disturbances because of troubled personalities; inner discords need outer discords; these involve polemics, and polemics may give a moment's peace within. The most troubling of all troubled people are those who can endure no constraints, limits, or authority, and who therefore in the name of liberty keep pushing toward disorder. Without knowing why, they cannot endure public order, however rationally created; their own wills are to be the only determinants of action and policy. They are a more serious threat to department welfare than the well-adjusted operator, who always probes for advantages but never thinks of dressing them up in high principles. He will let summer school die on the vine rather than be the instructor you desperately need, but if it suits his interests to teach in summer school, he will expect you to stay up nights squeezing him into the payroll. For him, too, a reader is a status symbol; so he will try to inflate his enrollment to make it appear that he has a reader coming.

But against both troubled disturber of the peace and untroubled operator we can balance the good man. He has a double-reader coming but teaches so hard that he reads all the papers himself. There is the talented man with a conscience who will say, "If the department needs me, I will do it." There are teachers who also write instead of using classroom demands as an excuse for not writing; there are well-known scholars and critics who also teach well instead of using their writing as an excuse for teaching halfheartedly or haphazardly. There are intelligent and objective men who think about department problems rationally and with a keen sense of institutional well-being. There are distinguished and less distinguished people who are not self-absorbed, who are driven neither to flattery nor contentiousness, and who can be counted on for even routine services to the department.

If I devote fewer words to these, it is not only that they are fewer in number than one could wish but that they provide no problems. The chairman needs to be reassured that they exist; they amply justify hope and faith. The others will tax his charity, and take most of his time. Here, as elsewhere, the chairman should be half a hero and half a coward. As a half-hero he will work himself up to facing difficulties and crises from which he might prefer to turn his eyes. As a half-coward he will be saved from taking on all the windmills in sight. For there is much, in problems and persons, that he must simply live with; hence he should not mistake half a loaf for a derelict's diet. Unless he wants to practice therapy full time—and I strongly recommend that he never touch it—he cannot do much about the more difficult types such as the nagger, the nonstop conscientious objector, the unconscious would-be dictator. He cannot do much about those who want the chairman to be a medley of Santa Claus, denatured Mephistopheles, and defanged divinity—one who praises but never blames, who is under contract to serve but is dismissible at will, who distributes manna but hands down no tables of the law. He will have to do some enduring. But beyond that the chairman can be an observer, a student, a learner, and, in his moments of happiest detachment, an ironic contemplator.

So much for general attitudes. Now for a few comments on combinations of attitude and action in more specific contexts. First, two obiter dicta on administrative procedures.

Nowadays there are no alternatives to conducting affairs democratically. Even benevolent Tudors are not fashionable. In academe, democracy is at its best when we have an aristocracy to start with, and we rarely do; we have to make the best of it. We can sometimes appeal to an undifferentiated democracy to transcend itself. This works better with smaller numbers of democrats. The larger the department, the more desirable that authority be delegated to an executive committee. The larger the number of people making decisions, the greater the influence of demagogues and of irrational men, especially the feelie-types who take every random emotion for a moral imperative binding on everybody else. The larger the assembly, the less of true candor, the less discussion of substantive issues underlying specific proposals, the greater the opportunity for polarization and schismatic sentiment

12

(which of course some types want).

The second rule for conducting affairs is this: by all means get an administrative assistant—a professional rather than a faculty amateur. By a professional I mean a woman (oh well, it can be a man if anybody is uptight about this) who probably starts out as a secretary but who has an executive sense that makes her invaluable. Somehow she remembers everything—rules, history, half-forgotten intentions, half-recorded actions. You will serve yourself best by giving her your confidence: keep her in touch with all that goes on, trust her imagination and good sense. The chances are that she will manage numerous things better than you would, that she will watch herself to avoid pushing people around, and that by taking responsibilities she will push you into the classroom and library where you should spend some time.

Decide whether you are a program man or a personnel man. For me appointments are the most interesting of all tasks, and I like to think that all else follows from them. Some very good men give primacy to programs, and think personnel secondary. Find in which way you act most spontaneously, and proceed accordingly.

Whether he makes policy by making appointments, or makes appointments to execute policy, the chairman must face certain facts of life. First, his appointive freedom is restricted by the type of institution he represents, by its tone and resources, and even its geography (for instance, I can't appoint people who want to be in private schools or small colleges or east of the Mississippi). Second, distinguishing among candidates is not easy. Recommendations are mostly written in a special dialect—double-speak, or marketplace Esperanto, or a kind of Braille—and it takes quite a bit of experience to translate it. I strongly advise reading folders aloud in committees, sometimes dozens of them on end; then meanings begin to appear. It takes time. And if you cannot trust recommenders whom you do not know personally, alas you often cannot trust those you do know. They take more pride in moving the goods than in pleasing the customer; they can always look terribly surprised later if you tell them that they sent you a boor or a bore, a slob or a sectary, or some kind of evangelist with a heart of gold and a brain of angelfood. A few, thank God, will level with you. As for the others, there are no rules. *Caveat emptor,* unceasingly.

If you are hiring a man who has a job somewhere else, beware of one who tells you how unsympathetically they have treated him. Three to one, being mistreated is his way of life, and you will be his next villain.

Get set for the yo-yo colleague who wants to do an annual bounce from your department to another because only perpetual motion makes him feel significant. You can't really explain to him that inwardly he fears his image would wither under continuous scrutiny by the same people. Resolve to live without him, or, if he is useful when visible, you may want to settle for half an oaf.

These days we hear much of planning. It can be overdone. There are real virtues in *laissez-faire* and *laissez-vivre*. The plan I value is less the rigid public blueprint than your best men's imprecise private images of a desirable state of things toward which, at whatever pace and by whatever means become possible, the department will keep moving.

Regard every decision as a precedent. What does it imply for other situations, and can you live with it? This is particularly desirable when you face regional imperialism in the department. Some sectors almost instinctively become pressure groups for infinite expansion, and under the banner of "excellence," "distinction," etc., push for ever more personnel, courses, budget.

Whenever you can, get writers to teach literature. They have an inside grasp of it as art that is needed to counterbalance the literary history, cultural history, and history of ideas that now have great play in English departments. Whenever possible let staff members teach outside their own fields; they will profit from knowing more, and visits abroad may help reduce field parochialism. Keep your own hand in teaching; the classroom may seem a haven from the department office, and sooner or later you will return to it anyway.

Finally, we have been told that we are in the midst of a revolution—an odd one that began in affluence but seems to survive in more threadbare days. The well-paid professor was no happier than the underpaid one, who now comes to the fore again. If his stirrings are a revolution, we can see its components—fraternitarianism, egalitarianism, and libertarianism. By fraternitarianism I mean collective bargaining, as yet so limited that we cannot tell how it will affect academic patterns and hence the role of the chairman. It implies egalitarianism, which may be a cry for justice, or a confusing of equity and equality, or, still more distressingly, an unconscious strategy by which the legitimate claims of equality are to be stretched into a thwarting of the claims of quality. Such an egalitarianism, carried to a logical conclusion, would ease the chairman out of his most difficult, his most significant, and his most satisfying function. It is libertarianism of which we have seen most—that perhaps final luxury of an affluent world which lies not in freedom from unjust restraints but in the belief that any restraint is unjust. The ultimate libertarian says to all, "Thou shalt not say 'Thou shalt not' to me"; any brake on my own will is tyranny. This view, of course, would eliminate chairmen except as they would

14

be content to be lackeys. On quite other grounds it is ominous doctrine, not only because it maintains a false view of reality but because if it spread from its present minority role it would beget a counter-falsity: it would lead to chaos, and the community would then sanction, in place of the chairman, an officer who would say, to all, "Thou shalt not" and "Thou shalt," and be obeyed.

But though I list difficulties, I want to underline my belief that the administrative life has much to recommend it. To describe its fundamental satisfactions I revert to my earlier terms: one rarely gets into this work unless it corresponds to some element of his own being, however defined, and it is satisfying to have that element exercised. Again there is the satisfaction of using power, however limited, to good ends. Furthermore we should never underestimate the value of simply keeping things moving in an orderly fashion, and the satisfaction of coping with the difficulties that this entails. When upper administrators such as deans and provosts complain of department chairmen, their grief is less over uninventiveness than over disorderliness, less over our failing to make big new ten-strikes than over our having things at sixes and sevens. If affairs have not gone backward during one's administration, one has some cause for pleasure. If he is lucky, they may even go forward. Though I have less faith in change—in either the possibility or the necessary beneficence of it—than do many reputable men, I in no sense rule it out as a source of pleasure to the administrator who accomplishes it. If he can innovate magnificently, let him glory in that; if he can here and there, ever so modestly, give a gentle upward nudge to the quality of things, let him glory equally in that. But perhaps the subtlest satisfaction is less in what he measurably does than in what he perceptibly is. He may be an image *for* that department; he is bound to be an image *of* it. *It* will tend in some degree to become what he is, and, knowing this, he may grow in the part, and present something of largeness of mind, some grace of demeanor and feeling. Conversely he will image what the department is, and, knowing this, he may intuit, amid all the obscuring accidents of its daily life, its latent gifts of spirit, and in turn so reflect them as to reveal the department in its noblest light.

Finally, there is some light for us in C. M. Bowra's 1967 autobiographic volume, *Memories 1898–1939*. Bowra, one of the great teachers of classics and, as such, a master of true relevance in the humanities, was considering the academic profession. He writes, "I gave thought to it and decided that a scholastic life must inevitably involve administration and would be all the better for it." In what sense, "all the better for it"? In two ways, potentially. The first is that the administrator may increase in knowledge. People, as we have noted, unconsciously reveal themselves to him—in more fundamental ways than they do to their colleagues; he sees more undisguised springs of action. (Academe is a prism that breaks original sin down into a spectrum of egotisms, from purple passion to green envy to red rabble-rousing. One sees virtues too, but somehow the vices are more educational.) He has more understanding of the human scene than he would have without the administrative vantage point; if he writes, he is likely to write more knowingly, perhaps even more wisely. "The better for it" secondly, perhaps, because as administrator the academic man has undertaken more, has elected to work harder, and may develop more than he otherwise would have done. He risks more moral pitfalls— those of self-pity, complacency, arrogance, blindness, and even injustice. But the conditions of his life should make him doubly aware of these, and he may undergo more of the discipline which gives form to a life. He may manage a little more of endurance, of the temperate acceptance of reality, of self-containment, of the adjustment to tasks, of an unsentimental charity. It is at least a possibility.

My hour is almost come. I feel like a guilty thing, too long unheeding the fearful summons back to the tormenting flames. But I hope that the old ghost's plaints do not make the night hideous or freeze young blood; that he does not seem one who has had poison put in his ear and has hence become too grouchy or jaundiced a witness. Above all I pray that this visitation is not to blunt thy almost whetted purpose. I point to no overwhelming tasks. Since the chairman, like the dean of men, no longer acts in loco parentis, he need not mete out penalties for incestuous sheets, reject the adulterate beast, berate the couch of luxury, or censure those who prey on garbage. He may leave them to heaven.

I summon you not to revenge, which usually means murder; not to fencing matches with doctored weapons; you need not detect spies who have bugged the arras, direct plays, guard against being shanghaied, pretend to be psychotic, or defend decorum in the cemetery. Instead you need only resolve to let Gertrude work things out in her own way, find out how to get along with Claudius, how to listen to Polonius, how to redirect the energies of Laertes, how to exercise restraint and avoid irony with Rosencrantz and Guildenstern, how to talk understandingly to Ophelia, and how to bring in Fortinbras as your administrative assistant. Think me then an honest ghost, more descriptive than prescriptive, intent on reporting all that goes on in academic Elsinore, but generally hopeful, envisaging, on the other side of difficulty, at least an iota of attainment and a sliver of contentment— no less than mortal due. I do believe it works out that way.

IN THE CLASSROOM:
READING, WRITING, TEACHING

2
Literature and Growing Up
The Ends of Literary Study

Some years ago, in a university in which I was then teaching, I had to help score several thousand English placement tests for freshmen each fall. This drudgery had one advantage for the scorer: he might be able to spot some of the better students and snatch them for his own sections—provided, of course, that he knew what the score was, that is, what the score meant. I soon learned that of the seven parts in the test, only two seemed to identify important qualities of mind (I do not speak of technical proficiency) that made the student especially desirable—namely, the two parts that were to test (1) his vocabulary and (2) his ability to read. You could forget about his spelling, grammar, punctuation, etc.; he might have high scores in these and still have only a mechanical or orderly mind. But let him have a good score in vocabulary and reading, and you had a mind that had begun to show liveliness, flexibility, and even depth. The owner of the mind was already moving toward that mastery of verbal symbols which is essential in a political order where wide communication has to precede and go along with all kinds of group action. But beyond the utilitarian competence, he was also pretty likely to be the better reader of imaginative literature. And for that reason, you instinctively felt him to be a little closer to general maturity than his fellow who had developed less skill or no skill in dealing with literature.

To say this much is to pose the general problem of the relation of literary experience to the achievement of adulthood (and, to continue the political reference, to the adulthood without which a democracy cannot survive). I trust this feeling that the good reader had come a little closer to maturity than the others. A skeptic might argue that instructor and student are only sharing a pleasure. But there are pleasures and pleasures; some are corrupt, some are cathartic, some are neutral, and some, I believe we may say, serve to "humanize" those who experience the pleasure. I believe that the pleasures of imaginative reading—the imaginative exercise under the guidance of the extraordinary and yet disciplined imagination which is the mark of the artist—are of that sort: that they help bring out a potential humanity, lead the individual toward his full status as a human being—in a word, help him to grow up. By growing up I mean the realizing of certain qualities or attitudes that are potentially present in man but that have to be cultivated if he is to become truly "human." I think, for instance, of the kind of awareness he has of himself and of human reality generally, and the kind of feelings he has: how closely do the awareness and the feelings correspond to reality?

Into the humanizing or maturing of the human being many influences must go, I need hardly say: many disciplines of the mind and heart. Here I speak of only one of these influences: the coming into a certain knowledge of humanity of which the literary imagination is an important instrument. The literary imagination makes it possible to know immediately and concretely, and with even a breathtaking fullness, what it is like to be a human being. It provides an inside, thoroughgoing experience of human reality that I will call a "feeling knowledge." It provides this feeling knowledge in two dimensions, in breadth and in depth. By breadth I mean knowledge of difference—of human beings different from oneself, of different impulses, different feelings, different intellectual and moral attitudes. One cannot respect difference without experiencing it, knowing it with that inside "feeling knowledge" that I believe imaginative literature gives. Too much of the time we pay lip service to difference while really acting as if the only virtue were sameness. We might avoid this inconsistency if we thought of difference not in terms of specific incongruities that are repellent or inaccessible to us but simply as the sum of all the diverse ways in which human nature manifests itself. This literary exploring of difference may be called vicarious experience; the term should not make us feel defensive. Most modes of daily life are inevitably so constricting that any vicariousness may be an enlargement of the living of which the individual is capable. Granted, it depends on what he's being vicarious about, or who with. Erotic adventures with the latest movie nudie may contribute less to his growing up than to his blowing up.

The literary imagination offers its feeling knowledge of humanity also in depth. Here I use *depth* to mean the additional reality that lies beneath the surface of an action, the double motive, the conflict of purposes, the clash of different values. Othello wants to indulge his revengeful violence against Desdemona, but he also wants to feel that he is acting justly, like a court. Cordelia proudly refuses to compete with her sisters in a verbal grab for Lear's royal estates, but by this act of honorable pride she gives the game up to her calculating sisters and makes possible dreadful suffering and many deaths. Oedipus the King wants to detect the hidden crime, but he also wants to retain intact his pride in his intelligence and his sense of personal integrity and royal power. Conrad's Lord Jim wants to act nobly and gloriously, but his very dream of heroism is undermined by his instinct for self-preservation. George Eliot's heroes—Tom Tulliver and Adam Bede—want to be good men, but in their pursuit of the good they can become hard and overbearing. Robert Penn Warren's heroes act in the name of an ideal and yet find their actions contaminated.

The human being to whom imaginative reading gives a feeling for and a knowledge of such duality in motive and experience is on the road to that awareness of human reality which is one way of fulfilling his own humanness. For it is not mature, and it may even be anti-human, to know human beings only in terms of a very simple black-and-white view of their moving impulses and of their desire and fulfillment. The more simply I can think of human truth, the easier it is to drop people into handy compartments, to make them conform to rules that suit these compartments, and above all things to deceive myself about what I am up to. In other words, the sense of human complication which is one gift from literary experience is an approach to self-knowledge, to seeing oneself in perspective, to recognizing one's doubleness of motive without falling into the opposite extreme of regarding all appearances of good as contemptible self-deceptions. Surely a student cannot work through such self-deceptions as those of Macbeth without having a door opened, if ever so narrowly, on his own share in human self-deceptiveness.

Gaining perspective on oneself is, alas, not quite so easy as saying "Know thyself" to someone else, and it would be no service to literature to intimate that it will move in quickly to solve what has long remained almost insoluble. For the quest of perspective or maturity obviously has to buck a number of powerful forces. First, there is a limiting concept of the human being that has a large but unacknowledgeable influence in American life. Second, there is a decided disinclination to self-knowledge which knows no national boundaries. Third, there is an equally extensive weakness for certain self-protective patterns of feeling that fog up the perspective. And finally, there are certain questionable ideas about the nature of a democratic order. I will look at all of these, but most fully at the third.

The Ghost on the Ramparts

A few years ago a student of mine in freshman English wrote that he was going to get ahead in life by, as he put it, "selling himself." He had so little perspective on himself that he did not know that he was talking a dangerous slave language, that is, reducing himself to a non-human commodity that could be molded into whatever the market would buy, nor was he willing to be persuaded that this was true. He was strongly under the influence of that antihuman element in our culture which wants to view man merely as an economic unit. That element cannot help resisting the kinds of imaginative activity which will enable a man to know that he is taking the part of a slave. That danger is less evident now than it was a decade earlier (it has been superseded by the danger of visionary utopianism, another kind of bait for the naive), but it won't take much change in the social climate for it to surface again.

Second, the young man's road was blocked by his share in our human tendency to fight off self-knowledge. For my young man literary experience meant only contact with popular literary and art forms, where human conduct is normally so stereotyped, so fitted to naive expectations, that its effect is to deepen and confirm ignorance of oneself. I wish not to give out with one more blast against commercial fiction and movies but to note factually the obscurantist quality of art in which we always identify ourselves with an obvious good (be it the defense of order or the rebellion against the way things are) and the good always wins. In that realm there are no ironies of character, no disconcerting depths; the hero suffers no inner surprises and no real disasters. In popular art Oedipus is secure, all of a piece, unchallenged in his superb self-confidence; he unfolds the crime, roots out the plague, and finds wrongdoing only in others. Thus we stay cozily young and ignorant. Though less cozily, perhaps, we stay just as young and ignorant by knowing another stereotype equally without ironies of character or disconcerting depths—the sex show that impedes growth by being too simple and easy and keeping the imagination lazy.

In fact one of the wonderful ironies of our culture is that on the one hand we proliferate an enormous and unprecedented popular art which is founded on the individual's passion to remain ignorant of the facts of psychic and moral life; while on the other hand we proliferate an enormous and unprecedented family of professions supposed to supply us with self-knowledge—vocational counseling, marriage counseling, personality testing, aptitude testing, psychological consulting and advising, and the vast brotherhoods of psychiatric activities, from mental health seminars to psychiatric social work to psychiatry for all income groups. On the one hand our technology encour-

22

ages mass habits of self-disguise; on the other we strain our resources to create habits of self-inspection.

Besides bucking the economic view of man and the general human addiction to self-ignorance, whether through self-protectiveness or sheer laziness, the quest of perspective through imaginative literature runs into a third difficulty—namely, the fact that we all want to go on not only *thinking* but also *feeling* in the same ways we have always felt. Feeling is habit-forming, and in art this leads to second-rate literature, by which I mean the literature of habit, printed dope sold across the counter at any drugstore. W. H. Auden argues that second-rate literature makes the reader say, "That's just the way I always felt." But first-rate literature makes him say, "Until now, I never knew how I felt. Thanks to this experience, I shall never feel the same way again." To learn to have, and to live with, new feelings, puzzling feelings, even disturbing feelings, is one way of growing up.

Without the correctives supplied by good literary artists, even our so-called "good feelings" can get out of line. To make this point, let me pick up my basic phrase, "feeling knowledge." By this I mean the insight that is possessed at once through the mind that discerns the general or formulatable truth, and through the emotions that accompany our participation in the specific human actions that literature presents. This full knowledge falls between the general formulae of organized knowledge and the particular masses of unorganized experience, and it draws something from both of these at once. Insofar as it has an intellectual aspect, we might think of it as "philosophical"; insofar as it is not intellectual or propositional, we may say that we possess it through "sympathy" and "understanding." Now, though both of these words imply a kind of knowing that is essential to maturing, the trouble is that both sympathy and understanding can fail to jell and can become simply soggy self-indulgence. We can get a crying jag from, or get blind drunk on, feeling that is not properly aged. I can think of four forms of sympathy which, instead of being a sensitive perception of what humanity is, degenerate into nothing but a pleasurable exercising of our simplest emotional machinery. One of these is to "understand" the cause or source of a human action so thoroughly that we forget the quality of the act; we know so well why poor Wilhelm murdered his wife that we forget that he murdered her. The opposite, but equally popular, form of sentimentality is self-indulgence in outrage and indignation; everywhere we see wrongs that we demand, righteously and angrily, to have put down. *We* always feel rightly; those *others*, wrongly. As a character says in Christopher Fry's *The Dark Is Light Enough,* "Any side can accuse the other / And feel virtuous without the hardships of virtue." What an admirable definition of this kind of sentimentality—"feel virtuous without the hardships of virtue." It is the moral trap on the course of every reformer, as we have learned only too well in the 1960s and 1970s. The third form of sentimental sympathy lies in the quick material charity which conceals a deep self-satisfaction; in the happy handout paid for by gratitude; the easy giving of *things* may be without adult sympathy, may be condescension sugarcoated with a tip, may be the front for a warm rush of self-congratulatory feeling, rather than the interplay of discrimination and emotional response which is at the heart of mature understanding. One might even work for another and still have it too easy; as Meredith's Lady Blandish says, "bodily fatigue . . . is the vulgarest form of love." Another Meredith quotation can introduce the fourth form of overeasy sympathy. "Sentimentalists fiddle harmonics on the strings of sensualism." But more recently we don't even require the intermediate labor of fiddling harmonics: we take sex and all the physiological phenomena straight, and apparently believe that we are entering a new era of understanding. But we cut ourselves off from all the difficulties and complexities that are essential to real understanding.

Considered in relation to knowledge, popular literature is a powerful strengthener of self-ignorance; considered in relation to feeling, popular literature simply serves to make us sure that we love and hate and feel virtuous according to conventional rules that ignore the complexity of life. But literature of quality ministers to sympathy and understanding without making them too easy and without getting sloppy about it. It engages sympathy, but keeps the object of sympathy in full perspective. It elicits at once warmth of feeling and coolness of judgment. It does not merely set us afloat on a wash of feeling, which is the way of sentimentality, or set us up high and dry on the judgment seat of principle, which is the way of lecture and homily. It draws us in but it holds us out; even while we are empathically engaged, we remain contemplative onlookers.

Take the central action of *Pride and Prejudice,* the clash and the love affair of Elizabeth Bennet and Darcy. Surely every reader is drawn into an immediate sympathy with Elizabeth the heroine; yet Jane Austen does not permit this sympathy to become sentimental by being no more than a gush of feeling for a person who is right but wronged. The reader is compelled to recognize that Elizabeth is also wrong and has to be righted. The very warmth of her family loyalty leads her into misconceptions, unfairness, injustice, and, above all, moral complacency. To understand her fully is to have an experience in the training of human feeling that should make for adulthood. Darcy also contributes importantly to this training, for the portrait of him compels the reader to go beyond the rather immature pleasure of hating snobbery (most of us resent only the snobbery of others, but cling devotedly to our own in the conviction that it is our critical acuteness in action) and to take into account also his ability to see both others and himself sharply.What we feel through him, even before we place it intellectually, is the double direction which pride can take in the human being—becoming, on the one hand, snobbery and arrogance, and, on the other, sense of responsibility. If with Elizabeth we begin with what we might call simple sympathy, and find this made more mature by the judgment of her which we must make, with Darcy we start as distant, unfriendly judge, but find our simple judgment made more mature by the understanding sympathy exacted of us by his emerging moral quality. In this respect how nicely he is contrasted with Elizabeth's father, the sharp-tongued Mr. Bennet, whose ironic observations at the expense of his not-very-bright family we invariably join with in enthusiastic sympathy. But then we are forced into a revision of feeling. For we recognize that his delightful irony is made possible by his distance from his family, and that it is this very distance which under the stress of a practical crisis takes the form of irresponsibility.

What looks in some ways like a very straightforward story, I am trying to say, is a subtle trainer of feelings away from sentimental self-indulgence—simple love and hate—toward an emotional grasp of human reality. This discipline of feeling, if I may so call it, is managed in a different way by Shakespeare's treatment of Falstaff. If we look at Falstaff only in the light of principle, we are pretty likely to condemn him as a lying and brazen phony, as critics have done. If we regard him only with sympathetic feeling, we are pretty likely to become totally immersed in his humor and vitality, as other critics have done. But Shakespeare does not permit a careful reader the comfort of either of these simple and limited attitudes. On the contrary, I believe, he compels us to be joyfully at one with Falstaff, and at the same time to reject him. Unless one were a pedantic moralizer, it would be impossible not to feel the contagion of that exuberant, witty, and zestful personality; and unless one were sentimentally unbalanced (which is more frequent than being mentally unbalanced, and much more dangerous, because more likely to be taken for a virtue), it would be equally impossible not to identify his ethical carelessness and his scandalous irresponsibility. To come to grips with that full personality made up of coexistent forces that drive us to contradictory responses is to be inducted into some understanding of humanity, or at least into the exploration of its perennial problems. But surely it brings us into a sharper awareness of ourselves, of the Falstaffian in ourselves: of all that laughing, juicy energy, tricky and yet animal (that is, both buoy-

25

ant and cynical), that has as yet found no guidance but that of immediate self-interest; in a word, of the core of that youthfulness which is a good some of the time, some of which is a good all of the time, but which, as a total recipe for existence, must find some leavening or be set aside for more durable forms of the human confrontation of life. To place Falstaff should be a step in growing up.

What I am trying to do, really, is to set down the ultimate ends that I think I should be serving as a teacher of literature. I can't prove that literature works as a ripener of knowledge and feeling; above all I can never prove that any single work has such and such an effect. If literature is, as I believe, a maturer of humanity, that value is the sum of a continuous experiencing of books. The more that experiencing goes on, the more it should contribute to the flexible but penetrating awareness of the human situation, sometimes gay, sometimes grave, that we call wisdom.

If I am not stating demonstrable propositions here, I am really talking about a faith. I would guess, in the first place, that a teacher of literature at any level would need some such faith, whether its creed include these or other articles, that literary study achieves something positive and substantial.

If he disbelieves or is apologetic, he is obviously lost. If he secretly thinks that literature isn't quite "real" or up-to-date or practical, he is lost. Or he may have positive beliefs that don't go deep enough. If he thinks that literature is simply a direct ally of good citizenship or good behavior generally, he is lost. If he thinks of it as a dainty dish to come only at the end of a solid meal of a more fundamental nourishment, he is lost. He is lost, too, if he thinks of it as the specific vitamin that produces highbrows, as the caviar of artists and other special souls, as the Waikiki Beach of those who don't have plane fare, or as the costume jewelry that goes with what the culturally well dressed person wears. And he is lost if he thinks that the only literature of contemporary interest is that written in the middle of the twentieth century; this provincialism of time is worse than the pedantry that values only the past. The cult of the present, of being up-to-date, is the plausible, and often seductive, false front of the very thin philosophical idea that nothing is permanently true and that all the seeker after truth can ever do is to hang on to the popular fashion of thought at any given moment. In education this idea appears as an insane craving for novelty in the curriculum, and it is related to the dominance of methodological study and emphasis; the methodologist is divorced from substance, is unable to believe in it, is free to pray "Oh, Lord, let me find something new" and to go on goldberging new methods and new periph-

26

eral studies that continually erode away the solid and permanent core of things to be known. One can be a teacher of literature only by being committed to a belief in human constants which reappear, in whatever challenging diversity of dress, in all periods. The very diversity of dress may be of some advantage to us who are trying to ripen students, for the surface unfamiliarity may help reduce the exclusively emotional involvement that can make the literary experience only a state of heightened excitement, make it all feeling and no knowledge. The more mature the work, the more it is, or is capable of being made, contemporary, and our job is to find the contemporariness, that is, the human constants that lie beneath all the different forms, styles, and idioms. And we have to believe that our students, as potential human beings, are capable of responding to the images of themselves and their kind—to their differences and their new depths—as they are refracted in the multiple mirrors of literary artists.

The problem of how we get them to look into the mirror is a tough one, but we can never escape a commitment to try to solve it. For one thing we are lost if we surrender unconditionally to the popular "doctrine of interest," which says in effect that we can work only through whatever the student is already interested in doing or reading, be this the principles of fishing, the cure of the carburetor, the reform of the draft, or the latest ecological exercise. But it is no further from no reading to good reading than it is from, say, flies and rods to Caroline Gordon's *Aleck Maury, Sportsman,* or from souped-up motors to the sharp-minded chauffeur in Shaw's *Man and Superman.* The idea that knowledge follows interest is a scandalous half-truth; I suggest that it is a better-than-half-truth that *interest follows knowledge,* that what we are interested in is what we know something about. If a student knows very little about anything but sports and hot rods and the most recent musical vogue or cosmonautical adventure and hence is interested in few of the large subjects in which he is capable of being interested and in which grown-up human beings have to be interested—if such a youth is to be encouraged to announce what he isn't interested in and to believe that what he isn't interested in is a good guide to what he shan't study, the game is up. What's more, it is morally questionable to let an ignoramus think that the lack of interest which results from ignorance justifies an infinite prolongation of the ignorance. Interest isn't, like hunger or sex, instinctive; it is created by man's increasing contact with the world around him. It is a current generated by the friction of experience, and that friction needn't be a lucky accident or something that we hope will just happen some time. It can be induced and ought to be induced; i.e., there are things that people should be, and must be, interested in. We have to bring literary experience to the

27

young, and I think we can believe that for most of those with normal human equipment, the contact with what they need to be interested in will generate a workable modicum of interest.

This is the *push* method. Besides this, there is a *pull* or suction method. When the father of Montaigne the essayist wanted to encourage his son to read the Latin poets, he told the young man that he could have free rein in the library—except for those books on the top shelves that were not suitable for a boy of his age to read. This was the Latin poetry section of the library, and under this stimulating prohibition, Montaigne put himself through a good course in classical verse, and not in translation, either. Could we make some use of the forbidden-fruit principle, leading children into temptation to deliver them from the evil of ignorance? This would take some ingenuity, since the departure of censorship has left us with little operating room for the forbidden-fruit principle. However, mankind needs taboos for his own mental health, and perhaps we could slyly attach an air of the not-quite-permissible to the works we really want read. We jest about having made education too easy, but the jest conceals a point. When we seek new ways to corrupt the ignorant with the vice of learning, we may want to restore something of the old way of making it not too easily come by.

Until we commit ourselves to such machinations, we will continue to lead the colt to water; if we cannot make him drink, we can at least hope that in time he will get thirsty. (There is, of course, an occasional camel in horse's clothing.) All our homes need to learn what many libraries have learned—to leave books lying around, tempting the passer-through, teasing him into an exercise of freedom. When our son, now a high-school English teacher, was a high-school student, he picked up *The Adventures of Augie March* in this way; he would not duplicate now the eyebrow-raising that his teacher did then. If the loss of some taboos is good, we now have another problem: to make available the taboo-free writing by good imaginative writers so that it can compete adequately with the brave dirty-word clichés of the dead-end word-mechanics who can produce taboo-flaunting printed pages without any imagination at all. Here the danger is that of the too-easy thing. Beyond that, however, we need to keep in mind that it is not only a little knowledge which is a dangerous thing; all knowledge is a dangerous thing. At any time it may lead to disgust or shock or cynicism or revolt or the illusion of knowing more than one does or the trying vanity of the precocious brat who wears his reading list like a football letter or a diamond ring or a purple heart. But knowing too much too soon is a lesser evil than knowing practically nothing too long.

28

In days when whatever we do in school is mistakenly supposed to have some immediate and tangible bearing on sociopolitical life, we should take a brief look at the role of literature in our society. I suggested earlier that there are four obstacles in the way of the humanizing experience of literature. The fourth of these, which I now come to, I called "certain questionable ideas about the nature of a democratic order." I am prepared to argue that the kind of literary experience of which I have spoken seems to me to be necessary to nourish the democratic imagination. Though democracy, that abused concept, is sometimes used to imply a mode of life in which the commonplace is both expectable and gratifying and in which the very idea of standards of distinction seems pretentious, democracy, it seems to me, cannot claim a genealogically sound kinship to reality unless it is based on the supposition that a majority of men are capable of learning the kind of discrimination that will tend to give the good and the true some survival value amid the hurly-burly of events. It does not matter very much whether many people simply get what they want instead of just one person getting it (monarchy) or a few persons (oligarchy) or a special class (aristocracy); it does not matter, that is, if "what they want" is regarded as the sole end, without reference to the quality of what they want; the chief justification of democracy would seem to be that the majority are more likely than one, or a few, or a special class, to want the right thing—the thing that preserves and strengthens rather than the immediate and transitory gratification. This is really a fascinating and daring vision—the vision of the multitude as the true abiding-place of socially and morally creative discrimination. And after this preliminary definition, we can ask: what is the relation of the teaching of literature to this vision? Or, as it is sometimes put, what reading is suitable for a democracy? The answer is this, I think: that any literature is good for a democracy which contributes in any way to powers of discrimination—to a perception of the realities of human action, of the impulses and values that human action embodies, of the kind of individual and group choices that diminish and destroy or that create and conserve. That is the business of reading in a democracy— to minister to the powers of human discrimination. This is simply to say that any mature literature which is suitable for any mature or potentially mature audience is suitable, and desirable, for a democracy. All this seems terribly obvious; does it really need to be said? Perhaps not, and if not, good. Yet I have the uncomfortable feeling, from what I pick out of the air, that it is sometimes thought that we should be resigned to democracy as the political and social form of an extremely limited humanity whose main symbol is the grab bag, and that therefore the proper reading for a democracy is something "practical" (whatever that means), or topical, or local, or familiar in raw material, or political-propagandistic, or not too hard, or not too old, or not too "pessimistic" (whatever that means), and above all things not concerned with a monarchic or aristocratic order where life is artificial and rarefied and has no relation to the solid and earthy realities that we sturdy democratists live by. That is not only nonsense, but dangerous nonsense. If seriously applied, it would cut from our reading not only most of the profound works of world literature, but innumerable works with the difference in perspective necessary to modify our own complacency and provincialism. I am shocked, for instance, by some of the attitudes to Henry James; indeed, even in a graduate seminar on James that I happen to know about, a number of participants seemed to feel that James study was perhaps an acceptable academic exercise but really had no tangible relation to the basic realities of our own day—as if James's insistent preoccupation with states of consciousness, with conscience, with moral perception and reality could ever be unrelated to any kind of mature human existence. We have a dangerous totalitarianism of our own: it is the totalitarianism of subsistence (it may be called "subsistentialism"), by which the totality of life consists of making a living and then of making more of a living, but never of making the most of living. But the totality of life goes beyond making a living and includes other things which we will ignore at our peril. If we were seeking an insight into the relation between the personal and the political ideal, between individual passion and organization sanction, I do not know to what better source of feeling knowledge we could go than James's *The Princess Casamassima;* or if we were concerned with the relation between the personal and the social ideal, between the instinctive and the dogmatic, than *The Bostonians;* or if our problem were the modes of good and evil, than *The Turn of the Screw.* (Incidentally, Eric Voegelin's discussion of *The Turn* in the *Southern Review* for winter 1970 should put the significance of that work in a serious new perspective which has been badly needed.)

In brief we need to escape from a popularized form of thought according to which all life is felt chiefly as a perpetual negation: as a battle against certain entrenched and repressive political, social, and philosophic interests. This rasping negativism of attitude is widespread enough so that, in one form or another, one is constantly running into it. It is ultimately responsible, I think, for misconceptions of James as well as for other untenable literary ideas, such as the idea that there is no relevance to our own lives in literature written in other political and social frameworks and therefore not at all concerned with subsist-

30

ence, democracy, rights, and the elimination of evil from life. But the time of writing and the external structure of life are of little importance; what counts is the insight into human reality. Of that we can never get enough, especially when our problem is not to break down but to build up. By its nature literature should be one of the allies of the human imagination in its constructive and reconstructive roles. If it can contribute to the growing up of the individual, perhaps it can do the same for a society. That result will not be amiss.

3
The Full Man and
the Fullness Thereof
Printed Page versus Sound and Light

In a more nearly ideal academic world no one, presumably, would think it necessary to say that there is something to be said for reading. But some of us have begun to wonder whether, in an age which takes increasing pride in electronic machinery of all kinds, the printed page is not in danger of becoming an archaeological curiosity. To use this phrase is not to adopt a tactical hyperbole. Readers of the *New York Times,* for instance, were able to read, in the spring of 1969, about a group of writers—yes, under thirty—who said quite candidly that they had given up reading. They only went to the movies. It is an extraordinary phenomenon—writing for others to read but refusing to read what others write. Perhaps it is a phenomenon of selflessness—giving one's self away to others but never nourishing or restoring that self. Of course a less generous observer might interpret differently. He might see, in this all giving and no receiving, a traditional ailment—a way of playing god. Or nonreading might seem only a venial slip, rather common in romantic days of genial trust in whatever pops or pours out from within. Ben Jonson describes it in commenting on the poet who learns "only . . . of himself"; this self-taught maker, Jonson says, "confesseth his ever having a fool to his master." The nonreading writer might, by his example, have an unusual educational impact on his readers: he might turn them into nonwriting nonreaders. To canvass these alternatives is to take ourselves right into Sartre's *No Exit,* where an absence of books is one of the defining characteristics of hell (the characteristic destination of the man who would be god).

If this tale of presumably literate people who go to movies but do not read is representative, then we have a problem. But I find no confrontation at all between reading and electronic experience as long as they are supplementary and not competitive. In our day we have plenty of time for both—in life generally and on the campus. A real issue arises only if the electronic begins to supplant reading—in the culture or on the campus. We do not have plenty of classroom time for both, and we should be concerned only when reading and the use of reading material get shortchanged. I in no way challenge the pedagogical use of electronic materials when and where it does something that reading cannot do. I do lament the diversion of time, in college and university literature classes, from the printed page to records, tapes, films, and the like. This development shows an unconscious distrust of reading, and a failure to grasp the value of the complex discipline it affords. Hence I tend to be a little offish when I see an advertisement captioned "Games + Movies + Records = a New Kind of Education," for I suspect that we get, not education, but games, movies, and records: the means become ends in themselves.

Insofar as the electronic is a threat to the printed page, either in the culture or on the campus, its position gains strength from three habits of thought that are strong with us. They are summed up in three words that in common usage do not denote neutral entities but connote good things to be admired or sought after: the words *change, experience,* and *gut reaction.* Let us look at the impact of these; as we do so, we may also act as the defense attorney for reading.

Change is a magic word with us, and it may seem mad to have doubts about it. For we all know that change will take place, whether we welcome it or just endure it. What is bad is to assume that change is always good, that we are the better for it, and that passion for it is the hallmark of good guys. Our most characteristic mode of change is to technologize and specifically to electronicize what we once did by hand, body, mind, or imagination. This may be splendid, or regrettable, or something of both. It is not always easy to distinguish changes which are beneficent from those which are not. Hence we tend, in a few cases, to resist stubbornly or, in more numerous cases, to fall in with the powerful dogma that change is always an improvement. Since the movement from reading to the electronic is a change, we tend half-consciously to go along with it as a good thing.

A more central problem in the pressure of the electronic upon reading is revealed by the key word of a professor of English explaining why he devotes class time to tapes, records, and films. He says, "I want the kids to have the experience." (Note the effect of "the kids" itself: it transforms pupils into tykes, learners into circus-goers). "The experience" is the key. Subtly this particular kind of experience tends to become the sole experience, as if the audio-visual were the real thing, and reading were either nonexperiential or not significantly experiential. No one, of course, can oppose the kind of aesthetic experience offered by a poet's reading, an actor's presentation, or an electronic reproduction of these (in fact, a poet's reading, since most poets read very badly, is hardly likely to seduce a reader from reading). The point is that we are deprived of something important if the audio-visual becomes the sole or chief experience and thus preempts the time and place for reading. For these are two different kinds of experience, and if we lose the one afforded by reading, we will lose something I do not think we can do without.

For one thing, we would lose our way into a very considerable part of the literary realm. While electronics may in time translate all literature into its own idiom, for the moment it seems largely restricted to poems and plays. So far as I know, it does not endeavor to present artistic nonfictional prose. There are, of course, plenty of films of long fictions, but these are essentially different works of art—useful as illustrations of the original but not substitutes for it.

But suppose there were always electronic options, what can be said for experiencing the work by reading the printed page? In reading we have one sense directly engaged, sight, and what we see is a set of arbitrary symbols that denote, of course, not only the worlds of all the senses but all the nonsensory or extrasensory worlds. To use a Platonic metaphor, we are at two removes from the reality being presented to us. But since our problem is not one of cognition, we need not be afraid of this intervening space. Rather it affords an advantage in aesthetic perception: it makes possible a partial detachment in which the critical impulse profitably resists the hypnotic force of the work. This is an important kind of engagement with the work. The key word is *resists,* and this does not mean *triumph* over: the value lies in a tension between two modes of response, between, if you will, disbelief and the suspension of disbelief. If disbelief actually triumphs, the result is a skepticism which voids the experience; if belief triumphs, we simply become slaves of certain stimuli. In reading, one is in the experience represented, and yet has a critical perspective on it; he may be enslaved, but he is also free. I do not mean that all the pressures designed to get one into the work should (in some way) be restrained or denied; the more effective they are, the more the work is given that ultimate term of praise—"powerful." But the stimuli brought to bear upon the recipient are aimed not so much at his sensory apparatus as at his imagination. The verbal symbols do not beat upon him like fragments of actuality but encourage and invite him to transport himself into many other realms of existence. He is drawn into otherness, whether for enrichment or understanding or sympathy or self-knowl-

34

edge. The value of this outward movement into other realities, or deeper movement into his own reality, is surely axiomatic. But in reading one is not experiencing total immersion; one is in the stream and yet out of it, suspending disbelief and yet practicing it, managing to be both participant and judge, or at least observer of the thing participated in and of the process of participation.

In contrast there is the kind of aesthetic experience that strives to resemble actual experience or even surpass it in impact and intensity. This happens when the verbal symbols, which make possible both distance and, by stimulated imagination, closeness, are replaced by sensory symbols that greatly heighten the immediacy of the experience presented and tend to make it surround and overcome us. In wide areas of art we can detect a tendency to imitate life, not by mirroring it, but by becoming it, with all the pungency, incoherence, disturbingness, and shock of an actual life of conflict. Some sound-and-light shows, one judges, are as overwhelming as battlefield experience. It is in this direction, I believe, that the electronic tends to take us, by a perfectly natural development of its own rich technical resources. For the seeing of words that leads us to imagine human action it substitutes the seeing of bodies in action. For the seeing of words that leads us to to imagine sounds we substitute the hearing of sounds. There would seem to be no limit to the extension of this direct sensory experience. Aldous Huxley suggested that it is only a step from the talkies to the feelies. We can surmise the arrival of the tasties and, more easily, the smellies. It may be possible to devise a kinaesthetic mode of experience: to have walkies as well as talkies.

All I am trying to do is suggest, and perhaps not hyperbolically, a drive in the aesthetic world itself away from the imaginative and interpretative and toward direct sensation and emotion, the physical responsiveness to strenuous, almost compulsive stimuli. The respondent is mastered by the medium instead of moving through it to the kind of mastery in which warm participation is mysteriously joined with cool detachment. Here, of course, I am describing an ultimate development, one that we may have to learn to live with. But however well we learn it, we will be in serious trouble if we do not retain reading as an alternative way into literary experience. In a 1969 essay J. B. Priestley remarks that "it would be disastrous if and when television-viewing entirely replaces reading for pleasure. There are signs already that some committed viewers and nonreaders, of all ages, are beginning to suffer from a blunting of imagination, a kind of curious new anaesthesia"—anaesthesia as the natural aftermath of the hyperaesthesia of electronic stimulation. This is exactly borne out by one of the non-reading writers in New York who says, "It's just easier to go to a movie and let it all wash over you." Wash, precisely: be drowned in it. For the ultimate effects of total sensory overwash, another writing nonreader says that every young writer knows "that he's more consistently moved by what he sees on the screen than [by] what he reads." What he records as a fact is really a debility: we may call it softening of the imagination.

He admits a craving for the "most powerful images" of the cinema. In this he illustrates the third of the three antireading forces that I have been surveying. The first is worship of change; the second is the passion for making aesthetic experience simulate actual experience; the third is veneration for what we call the gut reaction. This also helps push us toward the multisensory, direct-impact version of literary art. In some quarters the gut reaction tends to become an ultimate source of value. Historically, of course, we are compensating—actually overcompensating—for our nineteenth-century forebears' diffidence about the gut; to be sure that we are not as they, we try to keep our feet firmly planted in the gut. Note that this metaphor makes it silly to invoke the idea of discrimination by asking "Whose gut?" as if we wanted to make a choice among gut reactions. Gut is the great undifferentiated gut, the last-layer bottom of things, the fundament of brute commonplaceness, irresponsible and unquestionable. Gut reaction is a humorless age's heavy substitute for the belly laugh. That age is not likely to be very hospitable to reading, in which the gut is called on too, but no more than the other elements of personality that act as critics of the gut. Reading implies reflection, growth of understanding, widening of perspectives, modification of preconceptions. In reading we negotiate with another, and hence with our own, view of reality. On the other hand gut reaction means rigid faith in whatever ache, itch, urge, yawn, yen, letch, pash, or putsch pops up from a murky subbasement and passes itself off as *vox dei.* Hence, like any prerational fixation, it becomes nonnegotiable. Gut reactions, the intellectual pauper's substitute for taste, eliminate all labors of discussion, of negotiation. *De gutsibus non est disputandum.*

In our relations with reality we can think of a spectrum of multiple possibilities. At one extreme we are immersed in reality itself, living in pressures, tensions, drives, passions, engaged physically, socially, emotionally. At the other extreme we are disengaged critics: this is the world of detached analysis or of the printed page in its cognitive dimension—the prose of descriptive or analytical abstraction. Midway between these extremes is the reading of literature: it uniquely draws upon the activities of both extremes, making possible at once a plunge into reality and a separation from it, an empathic entry into the world and a nonpassionate observation of it, an imaginative participation in

36

polymorphous experience, and a maintenance of the partial exile where meanings may be grasped. In this view, reading is not a preelectronic make-do, a temporary practice appropriate to the printing phase of technological advancement, but an essential human activity, with an intrinsic function that cannot be superseded. Yet one can see its central position always subject to threats, as central positions are, from pendular swings at different moments of history when one extreme or another seems to have the better grasp of truth and hence draws the middle toward it. Much eighteenth-century literature—there are notable exceptions—feels the impact of the rational-critical-separatist extreme; the pressure of that extreme magnifies the abstractive and commentative and inhibits imaginative engagement. In our day, however, the center feels the opposite pressure: what we call life calls to art and says, "Be me." The art that responds to this call of the wild inhibits disengagement. It presses us to total responsiveness, sensory and emotive submission; to be overcome, dispossessed, in a literal sense panicked, that is, merged with all. What I am saying is that this general tendency of our age moves faster and goes further because of the electronic skills which are also characteristic of our age.

I have been drifting in and out of the classroom, but my main point has been that the substitution of electronic experience, in the classroom, for the study of the printed page is lamentable. It tends to reduce the amount of reading by creating a thirst for the greater immediate excitement of sound and light. It will curtail the time for the critical inspection of what is read that completes the reading process and makes for better reading the next time. The classroom is for criticism; the critical experience is valuable; and it cannot be wise to attenuate it by the substitution of sensory experience which the age already supplies in excess and which even the literature read is, in our day, eager to approximate or simulate.

Reading allows the recipient of artistic impressions much greater freedom than does a multisensory stimulation which tends to envelop him. It lets him be both a critical outsider and an imaginative insider. Besides, if he that runs may read, he that reads may stop. He may stop at any time—to assimilate, absorb, meditate, clarify, refresh, sharpen up or correct impressions, and, above all, to compare related passages, to discover connections, to perceive structure and form. These are the ultimate activities in the study of literature, and it is the printed page that serves them especially well. It permits a continual breaking off of continuity without an essential rupture of continuity, which is held on to imaginatively; while stopping a record or tape or film seems a barbarous breaking off of what by its nature is meant to keep going.

Finally we need reading, as I have said, for all the kinds of literature that do not lend themselves to sound and light. Here I want to stress especially the long works that are not amenable to electronic representation without being transmuted into something else—the epics, the long poems of many kinds, the long novels, the fictional and dramatic trilogies. On the one hand reading is the most interruptible of the experiences of art that go on in time; on the other hand it is the most extendable. On the one hand the pause that makes for refreshment or reflection does not damage the whole; on the other the whole is not circumscribed by the limits that seem inescapable in the audiovisual domain. With the printed page you can isolate the moment without really stopping the clock or ruining the hour; or you can go on for hour after hour, or for as much time as you have available, in one day or a series of days.

In works of length the printed page offers the on-going, prolonged imaginative engagement which is valuable in itself: an experience or even discipline in the long haul, the sticking with it, the evolving and inclusive vision; the having to go beyond the brief episode, the fleeting excitement, the quickly mounting tension, the fast-acting catharsis of love and hate. If literature is a form of knowledge, then that knowledge ought in some part to come through the large work that comprehends more of life, in its duration, with its variations of tone, its diversities of incident, its conflicts of thought, its multiple patterns of feeling and conduct—with all the roughness and contradictions of actuality concretely present, and yet in the end surmounted by a formal power that, in its long tension with chaos, has neither a factitious triumph nor a failure that invalidates art. Hence I like to think that the formed long work may act through the imagination to contribute to the formed life. Or, alternatively, the long exercise, the one that goes on, with whatever inevitable intermissions, from one reading to another, may itself enhance the competence of the imagination—to be discontented with the facile stimulation or the hasty conclusion, to endure the succession of contradictions, to embrace more readily those whole representations in which dualities and inconsistencies are ever present but never finally obscure the ordering vision of human breadth and depth. This is one way of saying that reading maketh a full man, and of trying to define the fullness.

For these reasons I hope that we do not divorce ourselves from reading. However, I am not proposing that we take a vow of chastity against the seductions of electronic enchantresses. We can perhaps get by with bigamy if we keep our different loves in the right places. I should be worried only if the electronic mistress were to drive us entirely away from reading, which has the virtues of the durable spouse, so that we gave it up entirely or deprived it of needed time in class. The electronic enchantress has an advantage over the printed page in our day because she appeals to that terrible fickleness in us which leads us to imagine that all change is a good thing; because she offers experience of a powerful new sensory kind and tries to make us think that that old homebody, reading, despite the durable and complex imaginative fare that she always offers, is a bit tepid and dull, and really does not provide experience at all; and because she tells us that that gut reaction which she evokes really gets to the bottom of things, and should be trusted, and not really modified by critical second thoughts. She has now helped create this new shaggy antireading type whom we may call, a little academically, nonlegistic man, the latest incarnation of neobarbarism. But that she is charming does not mean that she is sinister. Obviously she offers a great deal of pleasure. We can enjoy it, as long as we don't let it eliminate other very substantial and very durable pleasures. She is the kind of girl we should have an occasional date with, but not elope with.

4
Except He Come
To Composition

This is of course the medicinal part of the program, the penalty for general indulgence up to this point: first the sour mash, and then the sour note. The program chairman may have thought of me as a sort of living pill or a Pennsylvania Dutch uncle. It would soothe me to think of myself as a spiritual digestif, a Courvoisier for communicators and composition experts in the audience, instead of a commonplace bolus or a packet of verbal Tums. Of course I may seem more like a heavy pudding that is totally tranquillizing, or the final nut course that guarantees an epidemic of upset stomachs.

After I had accepted the invitation, I hazarded the guess that I might take a retrospective view. I could see myself in some pass, not a very high one, gazing to the rear once more, the last of the Woolley and Scott Mohicans, before turning and going over the hill. The professional plain behind me stretches quite a way. I taught what I suspect was my last section of freshman English in the winter quarter of 1970; I taught my first sections of freshman English in the fall semester of 1927. From 1927 to 1948 I taught freshman English in every term, often three or four sections, occasionally only one or two. Since 1948 I have taught one section every other year. I report this neither in self-praise nor in self-pity; for twenty years it was just the way things were; for another twenty I thought we tenured types ought to keep a hand in the toil and trouble that are often pretenure. At any rate my tour of duty extends from the handbook days when grammar, correctness, propriety, and even elegance—say on alternate Fridays— were the defining symbols of our faith, to the day when the symbols of communication, though like all symbols they may not enter into everybody's practice all the time, appear to be the free wheel, the

40

asyntactic rush, the expletive and interjectional props—I mention only "y'know," the short *uh* and the long *uhhhh*—and the fecal and genital clichés. (Here I am describing, not judging; some points might be made against the decorum implicit in either set of symbols.) My tour of duty, to use other terms, extended from days when no one really questioned freshman English and a lot of it was required, to days when a lot of people questioned the course, and little or no freshman English was required.

I am of two minds about this escape from Egypt, as some doubtless think it: I feel both relief and regret. I am sorry for this doubleness of mind, for I envy the world of clear thought where truth and false-hood, good and bad line up neatly opposite each other, and one can pick sides and be happy where the triggers are. But in my myopia I find myself stuck in a fuzzy middle ground where opposites may each be partly true, and good and bad embrace in such promiscuous en-twinement that it's difficult to shoot the one dead without maiming the other. But for simplicity's sake and time's sake I will spare you an account of my relief and try to explain only my strange regret.

I do know, of course, about two standard suspicions that are evoked by anyone who, when change has almost divine status, suggests that what has passed on is not all bad. He is likely to be thought homesick for lost authority, or just plain homesick. The former suspicion, I insist, is not valid if the lament for a lost requirement is sung by a de-partment chairman. If the chairman has an authoritarian temperament to start with, he is so used to having it quelled by colleagues that it hardly persists, even vestigially; he becomes docile by habit; he is, and even looks, housebroken. Anyway, the view that love of a require-ment is naughty is untenable. Having requirements or not having them is partly a matter of fashion; here, as elsewhere, fashions shift, often in response to little more than the sibling afflictions of ennui and neophilia. When life has been unrequired enough for long enough, re-quirements become fashionable again, and everyone thinks them not only not oppressive, but positively fulfilling. Then in time fulfilment becomes tedious, unruly passions yearn for a fling, and out go require-ments, with plenty of ad hoc morality dished up to speed their exit, and accusations of the authoritarian vice against anyone who tries to keep all doors from being torn off their hinges. Right now require-ments are out, and woe to anyone who comes up with unmodish words such as "ought" and "should." But requirements will be back, and the real problem is one of what may most profitably be required, or how a fashion may support nontransitory goods, so that we may be less time's slaves, always ready, when slapped, to turn to the other chic.

41

As for the suspicion of general homesickness or nostalgia: if a man can sigh for a past thing, he seems to be only lamenting the inconsiderateness of history and the thoughtlessness of time. Instead of revolving about himself as they should, history and time pass on indifferently and convert him from a pole of reality into a neo-Lot's wife, stuck on a deserted roadway and homesick for Sodom. I am aware of the danger of being thought a piece of inadvertent statuary looking the wrong way and facing the future with only a rueful rear. With more time I would rehearse John Crowe Ransom's meditations on the need of a vegetative component in life. But I will only note that antinostalgism begs two big questions: that everything has to change, and that all change is good change.

Now back from preliminaries to freshman English. In offering the course and in requiring it we engage in a certain kind of symbolic action which I would like to look at. The word *composition,* which I now use for the first time, is a very suggestive one. For the product of writing compare the word *composition* with the word *theme;* the root meanings in Latin and Greek are identical, and a comparison carries us into implications. A theme is literally a placing or a position—to be defended or advanced. To go from theme to composition is to go from position to composition, from adopting a stance to putting together; theme implies contention, composition peaceful settlement. There is much to be said for putting-together as an experience or activity. It is a modest prosaic cousin of Coleridge's esemplastic imagination, an achieving of oneness: a finding of such unities, small and contingent though they may be, as are possible in a world much given to the crying up of diversity. A putting together implies in some sense a resolution of discords, a removal of what doesn't belong, and a discovery of how to belong. In such a fitting together of parts, one cannot master all that one would, but one seeks a limited harmony, the agreement of parts in a movement toward wholeness. Agreement implies concession, compromise, the discovery of common grounds.

Our different uses of the word are revealing. For centuries it was a basic political term. Motley in 1860 wrote about an action's "bringing about some honorable composition," and Selden in 1654 of the "quiet composition of seditious tumults"; Hobbes two years later of the body "which is capable of composition and resolution." Honorable agreement; the settlement of tumult; the resolving of conflict—a coming to terms with counterforces, a subduing of oneself as much as of another, an acceptance of another as well as of oneself, a bargaining toward peace. This may sound too grand, but something of the kind has been at least implicit in the college composition business. A 1523 translation of Froissart has one ruler saying to another, "I desire you that we may abide in composition, that ye make us no war, nor we to you, the space of a month." Note the sensible hope: not eternal settlement, but a month's coherence instead of disagreement. Thirty years later, in 1553, the famous rhetorician Thomas Wilson defined composition as an "apt joining together of words in such order that neither the ear shall espy any jar, nor yet any man shall be chilled with over-long drawing out of a sentence." Historian and rhetorician inveigh against extremes that clash: make no war, the ear espy no jar. No war; no jar. What we symbolically supported in composition was the experience of striving for peace among the clashing thoughts and feelings, ideas and urgings that jangle in the personality before it has tried to form them up in a tentative oneness—in the treatise which is a kind of treaty.

I have been talking about the written work. But the written work is the working of the writer—and perhaps *in* the writer. Many of us have experienced the sense of being put together by the process of putting together. We have composed, and in a sense we are composed. *Composition* has roots that grow out in various directions; thus it calls our attention to relationships beneath the surface. It implies composedness in the thing made, and, in the maker, composure. It's a little risky to follow the root into another growth, compost, unless we remember that originally it was an organized mixture of fertilizing elements, a salubrious composition. And there's compote, where what is put together hints a composed flavor, and something of elegance.

I am toying, remember, not with formal intentions and measurable achievements, but with symbolizations. What I have seen symbolized in the composition process is the whole range of behavior implied in composing—bringing together, giving form to, ordering, compromising with difficulties both inner and outer, with self and with others: peacemaking. That composite of implicit values is one that I would be sorry to see fall apart.

We can see it falling apart, though, under the pressure of certain professional attitudes and styles that I have not heard much questioned but that I think deserve a question or two. Take the old cry against "schoolmarms" which has been echoing through recent corridors of time with a frequency and loudness that surpass its applicability and justice. It has an unseemly reek of self-congratulation; by it we point at sinners and rejoice that we are not as they. It's the free-spirit good guys against the rule-bound bad guys (and dolls). Granted, a rational ideal may beget rationalistic formulations; Francis Fergusson has pointed out that the well-made play is a kind of mechanized hand-me-down from the rational ordering of existence in the drama of the Enlightenment. But in antischoolmarmism there is an excessiveness that not only screams self-approval but hints at self-justification. I suggest that abusing schoolmarms symbolizes a stirring, a resentment against the kind of orderedness, the disciplining of the parts, symbolized in the concept of composition. Instead of the putting together of parts by order there is implied a simply rule-free putting forth of a something that is already there. This is a mode of writing that I will call the ejaculatory.

I leap from this widespread practice to a single event that I suspect is representative. Recently an applicant for a position wrote us an unusual expression of willingness to teach a considerable number of fields of literature. But he eliminated one teaching field—composition. In composition, he said, "I feel that I have done my time"—this after two or three years as a teaching assistant. I hope it is not only the perennial teacher of composition in me that raised eyebrows at the view of life implied in his words—the sense of a task to be avoided, not of a need to be filled, and hence of an obligation upon the instructor. He simply claimed a privilege. Implicitly instruction was for him not so much an ordering as an ejaculation.

The man who has done his time is only a cruder version of the type who wants private longings to determine curricular arrangements. We all know, for instance, the man who speaks of a teaching program in terms of "what I want to do." His want is not subject to criticism; rather it is a justification for the doing. The demand of personality replaces the demand made by an objective body of material. The contrast is between those who set out to teach it because, to borrow a phrase, "it is there," and those who want to teach it because it is here. The out-there versus the in-here. If the in-here comes from an intellectual giant, well and good, but giants are infrequent among us. Besides, giants tend to be attuned to metaphorical voices outside themselves; nongiants to trust to the inner voice, that often insidious seducer that assures us that what we want to do is what we ought to do. To shift to political metaphor: it is surprising to see, in a profession that generally votes Democratic, how much faith there is in *laissez-faire*, in public good as a by-product of unregulated private enterprise in the pedagogical domain. In this view the man who makes a course in American novel since 1930 into a kaffeeklatsch on six minor writers dear to his heart is not deemed to have let his personality rip and to have sabotaged the field. I will say more about him in the next essay.

Perhaps he teaches the six because he wants to write an article on them. This is another form of private enterprise: believing that one's own research profits justify delivering to the public some special goods as a substitute for what is listed in the sales catalogue. A subtler form of the profit motif is turning the classroom into an emotional gymnasium or playfield for the instructor, who can turn any text into parallel bars or trampoline for the display of feeling, or a punching bag to bear his intellectual blows, or a bow and arrow with which to shoot at favorite targets. Personal inner pressure overcomes the power of the text: the ejaculatory mode again. If he feels any need to make a case for this, he will come up with either or both of the cliché half-truths that so often are stand-ins for thought: he is being "relevant" or "doing his thing." In many quarters these clichés are not substitutes for thought but contraceptives of thought—little verbal pills or IUDs that block conceptual life, and sometimes have unforeseen side effects. Most talk about relevance simply begs the serious questions of the nature of relevance, the mode of relevance, and the object of relevance. It leaves us with the carcinogenic notion that immediate topical applicability is the end of all study and knowledge—a notion that will simply eliminate the field of literary study by rendering it subservient in turn to each of the public goings-on that seem from month to month to define reality. "Doing one's thing" likewise begs questions —of what the thing is, of whether it is final and unalterable, of whether it is worth doing, and, above all, whether it is good to do it. Rapists and murderers do their thing too. The do-your-thing doctrine has one especially dubious consequence. If own-thing-ism is an absolute, one says not "'Tis a poor thing but mine own," but "'Tis my own thing and therefore a good thing." Good things should be made available to others. As a wise observer has said of one own-thing-ist, "He not only wants to do his thing; he wants to do it to everyone else." And to say that is to put the finger on the sad kind of illness we often see today: the inability to know freedom except by compelling or injuring others.

These are not, I hope, only a random set of gripes. The common element is complacency and self-indulgence, and more than that, perhaps, naiveté: the unquestioned, indeed hardly articulated, faith that any urge, desire, drive, longing, need, whim that pops up or wells up within is an imperative which in pedagogy takes priority over any other imperative. It produces the ejaculatory mode of life. When we bring this style into the classroom, we are poorly equipped to deal with counteregotisms that wash in from the other side of the desk. What is more, we help beget, in students, the belief that there is some unassailable prescriptiveness in attending only to a current interest (relevance), doing what they want to do, doing their thing. Aside from production-belting out these clichés, often with a sense of metaphysical discovery, students come up with other gestures in the ejaculatory mode—for instance, the argument that grades are improper in

45

English because English is a "subjective" field. What saddens me is less the idea about grades, in which honest men may differ, but the view that the field is "subjective." In a way we have asked for it, for this kind of reduction of the field to dust particles flying out from our own fancies. Many of us, it is true, do labor continually at the genuine problem of identifying and defining the object that is there and the kind of claim it has on us. But too many of us do conduct ourselves as if the field were only a dusty projection from various private lives—one, of course, that can be blown away by the next big wind of fashion. If a field is only subjective, it can call forth only the casual exchange of undifferentiable opinions; this need not be institutionalized, for it goes on better in barroom than classroom. If what passes for knowledge is only opinion, what looks like freedom of opinion will have its unforeseen side effect: in the end one opinion will triumph over all freedoms—the opinion that is best organized, most attentive to purpose, and least scrupulous.

The doctrine of subjectivity is enchanting because it is gratifying: there is really nothing to challenge the opinion to which one's ego has attached itself. The same gratification underlies a couple of other lines of criticism in education—the anti-information line and the antistructure line. Classes, we are told, must not peddle information. There may be courses, I admit, in which a mechanical dissemination of data is the cardinal practice. But I am much more concerned about the opposite extreme, in which ejaculation, on both sides of the desk, displaces information on either. For anti-informationism loses sight of the fact that information is what we think with. The naive anti-informationist sets up a dichotomy of knowledge and thought, and he opts for thought. The big trouble with this may be put conveniently in Bunyanesque terms: Mr. Big-Think is only the self-image of Mr. Little-Know or Mr. Strong-Feel. Really he wants to stick to emotive habits and remain unshackled by information that might counter them. In this he may be either fool or tool. Then there is the student who complains that a course is too "structured." This is his way of asserting that what is already in him, unformed, changing from day to day, is a good thing and should not be tampered with, not subjected to shaping by formed knowledge. I am reminded of a phrase by Loren Eiseley, "For that without organization life does not persist is obvious." I suggest that a resistance to organization expresses not merely a secret attraction to chaos, which we all feel at times, but a singular aversion to life itself. Not that the antistructure man knows this. He believes that he is for life. But what he is really for is unordered bursts of energy and feeling, now this way, now that. He wants to stick to the ejaculatory mode, to be the ever-uncapped gusher.

46

The mode has its own rhetorical ploy: it appears in such phrases as "where it's at" and "get with it." We may call this the nonantecedential *it*. In days of sexual taboos the nonantecedential *it* stood for the unmentionable; in our day, when taboos are of a different sort (we always have taboos), the *it* stands for the unexaminable. It is literally a rhetorical device: it persuades us to ask no questions, seek no definitions, but buy a pig in a poke. *It* is what the loudest voice says it is at any moment, and compliance with that proclaimed reality seems the only permissible action.

The sense that the unstructured, uncriticized outburst from within is always something true and good is best expressed in the doctrine of sincerity, a rather handsome siren until one looks beneath the make-up. She has stripteased many writing courses. Her seductive line is that the teacher is imposing artifices upon the innocent child, and hence that the child is fighting back with his whole artless self. "This is just the way I am," he says. In a word it is better to be sincere than to be accurate and ordered. As with most such popular slogans, there is a false dichotomy: one may be sincere and accurate and ordered, or be sincere better if accurate and ordered. But the vice of sincerity justifies lack of second thoughts or even first thoughts; or of reflection, care, modification. Sincerity is worse when it is conscious; the consciously sincere man is in a snare in which he can't do a thing for himself. We all remember Sheridan's Lady Teazle, who is entrapped by consciousness of her innocence. Joseph Surface, her would-be seducer, points this out to her. He keeps asking her hard questions: why are you so thoughtless in what you do? So reckless in conduct? So imprudent? So impatient? And the answer always is, "Why, the consciousness of your own innocence." One might do the same with the beginning writer whose only rule is sincerity. Why are you so disorderly and uncontrolled? Why, the consciousness of your own sincerity. Why do you have so many clichés and secondhand thoughts? Why, the consciousness of your own sincerity. Why do you leap to so many easy conclusions, take so much on trust, ignore all the complications beneath the surface? Why, the consciousness of your own sincerity.

Another version of sincerity resisting structure and growth appears when a person says "This doesn't turn me on" and also feels sure, when he says it, that he is making a valid adverse judgment of *this,* and need do nothing more about it. Against that we have to place Gide's insight: "Culture begins only when we approach what we do not already like." The word *culture* is in disrepute, I know, for silly things have been done in its name. But whether we use these syllables or others, the value denoted is indispensable: the trained as against the wild, the tempered as against the raw, the aware as against the igno-rant. To remain closed to what does not turn us on at first is to stay raw, to reject the act of will, the imaginative leap, the growth of self by knowing the other. It is to refuse, among other things, the kind of inner move without which there can never be a composition of the races.

I have been harping on all the attitudes and fashions and key phrases that often seem to denote either virtues or timely procedures and yet still have the effect of making human beings forget their potential and stay put at some undeveloped stage because in self-will or self-indul-gence they resist modification. It is sad to see in students, yet I have been more interested in pointing to faculty attitudes that contribute to student foibles. In all this I have always been talking, even if indirectly, about two concepts of writing: writing as composition, and writing as ejaculation. In writing as composition I see a process of putting to-gether, of making concessions, finding agreements, seeking compro-mises, giving up something of rage and conscious rectitude, laboring toward the form or organization that is the natural channel of life, achieving, at best, a reconciliation—of selves and nonself—with bene-fits extending beyond the moment. In writing as ejaculation I see an assertion of personality, a justification of mood and moment, a trust in what one wants to do or thinks he wants to do, an uncritical accep-tance of one's thing and a sense that others ought to love it too, an absolutizing of transient concerns, a belief that one's idiosyncratic outrush is the equivalent of anyone's reasoned discourse, that an unde-fined *it* has a priority over knowledge and orderedness. In one we see a shaping, a molding, a moving toward an overall relation of diverse potentialities; in the other a jetting, a seizure of power by whatever self or psychic pressure group is most aggressive at the time, an accep-tance of the moment's actuality as final. In the one, composedness, in the other eruption; in the one, composure, in the other, excitement. Now I'm not at all against excitement; we have to live in it most of the time; but it is pernicious when it also controls those few hours a week when we ought to—must—try to improve on random impulses and emotions that crave to be their own justification. In the one, real-ization and formation; in the other catharsis. I'm not against catharsis either; the problem is only one of mistaking the study for the lavatory or the vomitorium. On the one hand we try to encourage growth by evaluation and control; on the other we practice therapy by emetic, carminative, and laxative, and we supply, or even become, appropriate receptacles. Hence perhaps the diary, which seems to be having some vogue as a classroom surrogate for critical writing. To a mind already

48

trained, I am sure, a diary may be highly structured writing; to an unformed mind, I suspect, it is little more than a casual sketching of flux. Paul Delany remarks, in his book on seventeenth-century autobiography, that a diary helped the writer achieve "peace of mind" by convincing him of the "inner experience of God's grace." I am afraid that having this conviction is not conducive to growth. Indeed, simply as therapy, I have a little more faith in writing as composition. I think of the words of Swift, talking of rhetoric: "By what kinds of practices the voice is best govern'd towards the composition and improvement of the spirit." In writing one uses one voice or another; with effort one may discover the voice that does make for composition and improvement of the spirit.

Composition and ejaculation. Let me close by shifting to Gallic metaphor. The difference is that between the French Academy and Mardi Gras. This is a risky image, for the academy is not everywhere in good odor; especially with Mr. Little-Know and Mr. Strong-Feel it is likely to seem only the original schoolmarm, and carnival the ultimately free secular Beulah Land. I hasten to add that I'm not against carnival any more than I am against excitement and catharsis; I suspect it only when it pops up all year round in classroom, study, and library. I suspect carnival even more when it makes like Lent, when it purports to be a reconstruction operation, when it becomes pressing and pleasureless and the revelers assail passersby for the good of both. To shift the metaphor from Paris and New Orleans to Vienna, one distrusts the id when it makes like the superego. At times it seems to be our new modern masquerade, and it subtly transforms All Saints' Eve from playing games to finding game. When the id is cast as superego, the free masquers, who purport to free us all, eventually turn into the Inquisition. When we get unstructured enough, eventually we get restructured, compelled by iddish energy from without.

The academy, French or otherwise, may fail badly: the pursuit of order may fall into rigidities, form into formality. But the ideal symbolized is civility, and civility is the ultimate victim of the I-want, I-turn-on, my-thing, carnival, id-powered style. Against civility we often set the cry from the gut. The gut reaction may be either a legitimate anguish of spirit or just a growl from the old Adam that hates even small progress toward being human; it may transmit a true cry from the soul, or an itch rising from the lower sole and seeking relief by kicking someone else. In its latter form it will insist on the ejaculatory mode. The mode will always purport to speak for free life, but it will generally coast on a stream of clichés and secondhand ideas. With an inner assurance of grace, it will want to give final authority to the personality of the moment. Hence it will tend more to moralizing than understanding, will turn away from humanistic civility and toward a strange puritanism. (After all, it is only two or three syllables from id to ideology.) The ejaculatory mode, paradoxically enough, also turns away from the humanistic in an opposite direction; on its aesthetic side it heads less for shores of light than for sun-baked beaches, less for the topless towers of Ilium than for topless hours at Hilo. Who can regret the topless hours? No one, I think. The only point is that, insofar as we are in search of a style, they are a little on the easy side.

John Ruskin has defined composition very aptly: "the help of everything in the picture by everything else." If we say the help of everything in the written work by everything else, we have a decent sense of agreement—of mechanical parts and of logical parts, of language and intention, of style and thought. This does not come easily. It implies a placing together by study; it implies negotiation and pacification, within oneself and with the world of thought. Hence when we reject composition or let it become ejaculation, we may well be performing a symbolic act far different from one more restless tinkering with the curriculum. In the words borrowed for my title, except he come to composition, a man remains un-put-together, more than usually troubled by the feuds within, and therefore a little more addicted to those without.

I hope you now remember the beginning when you were identified as an audience of patient youth listening to an elderly gentleman look backwards from a minor elevation just before going over the hill into some undefined beyond. I cannot know at this point whether you think the gentleman, who was supposedly only at a moderate elevation, is really way up in the air, or has come to such a pretty pass that he is having waking dreams, or is looking back fondly into a never-never land, or is just a little further over the hill than anyone, including himself, supposed. Any verdict seems to leave him subtly bound to some spirit of the past, impalpable but tenacious. And having acknowledged that, he must still plead for his presentness, and do it indeed by invoking a code word of modernity: relevance. To him, the relevance of the past is that it always tends, after whatever delays, to become the future. Thus you see one who may seem to be out after hours proposing that he is really ahead of his time, ringing in the old because it is almost new. He hopes that this paradox will not seem, after much sermonizing, a final affront. But if it does, he urges upon you your best nature as masters of composition and communication: be composed, not ejaculatory.

5
The Cult
of Personality
Hell's Spells

On his eighty-sixth birthday Somerset Maugham publicly congratu-
lated himself on his eschatological good fortune. He announced to the
press, "I don't have to face the prospect of eternal boredom in paradise." Mr. Maugham's modest disclaimer of spiritual merits is not
altogether original; in this, somewhat characteristically, he gives a
slightly different twist to a stereotyped posture. The usual gazer into
eternity puts it the other way around. He implies that he's been a bad
man. Things don't look good for him. He cannot expect to move up.
Ahead, in fact, it's all down hill. But then a glint comes into his eye:
"There's one thing about being damned. In hell I'll be with all the
interesting people."

This joyful prophecy, this cliché of self-contentedness, has a considerable academic currency, and it is humanists who are most addicted
to it. We need not peer too sharply over the façade of spiritual humility; we need not push our suspicion that the hell-happy professor may
be parlaying Milquetoast misbehavior into Faustian sin; nor need we
inquire whether his new doctrine of things-to-come is simply one
more outbreak of that titillating anti-Victorianism through which
Victorianism continues to claim our age as her own, at least her natural, child. All we are interested in here is the symbolic value of the it's-
so-interesting-in-hell pitch. When we picture ourselves as being eleva-
ted to a sort of high-class lower-depths café society, we are taking a
familiar romantic script and really giving it a new look. No longer are
we practicing old-line diabolism, upending the moral order in Byronic
or Blakean style, setting up hell as a school of liberty against ancient
tyrannies, hissing with new reverence, "Evil, be thou my good." No,
we are just exclaiming over what social fun it's going to be down there;

51

we are going to escape the doldrums of earth and be translated into infinite vivacity with damned interesting people.

The conventional infernalism has been aestheticized, and this is a symbolic action of the cult of personality. By the cult of personality I mean the substitution of aesthetic for intellectual, professional, or moral criteria. I am not talking here about the examination of art and literature, where aesthetic criteria are proper, but about certain social and academic habits. These reveal a penchant for being deflected from appropriate considerations and attitudes by what is "interesting" (or "attractive," "delightful," "charming," "magnetic," "absorbing"). I am not against the interesting, entrancing, enchanting, or seductive; but I want to note the inroads that, in an age of personality cults, these values have made into other domains. We symbolize this aesthetic imperialism by converting hellfire into gracious-living candlelight flickering on gay wits at brandy.

First, a heartening irony: as cultists of personality, we are inconsistent and even wilful. The personal attractiveness which we postulate in the dead and doomed, and which we apparently believe will be largely devoted to entertaining us, may be very irritating in the living and unjudged. When some colleague in our humanists' shop turns up with a displeasing use of the pleasing style, we dispose of him by calling him a "personality boy." If his personality goes on to become intolerably attractive to others, we puncture him with a still more reductive phrase: "charm school type." It would of course be too easy a cynicism to dismiss "personality boy" and "charm school type" as simply the unkind names for someone else's aesthetic success that may seem to us not firmly grounded in merit. The words embody, I am sure, a repudiation honestly meant. Predictably, however, human repudiations are not always impartial. We throw personality out the front door; but when it suits our purposes, or when our own personality becomes the issue, as I hope to show, we sneak it in a backdoor which turns out to be practically the whole rear wall of the house. When it is our own personality, we let it in and let it rip with all sorts of special privileges.

In our day it would be positively heretical to deny value, in any academic course, to the flavor of the individual instructor. The problem arises, however, when the whole course gets taken over by the flavor and turns into an unrelieved diet of vanilla, or even, as sometimes happens, of wormwood. This is always a possibility in the relations of instruction; all I am saying is that it happens oftener in a day of personality cults—that is, in a day when the "interesting personality" is so valued that it renders enchanting a grim cavern traditionally used to symbolize spiritual imperfections. Now when a classroom begins to take on the air of an ice-cream or scent factory, we soberer souls tend simply to turn on the student and grieve that he should sell his soul for that mess of vanilla (or of wormwood). But the fact is that he is not much different from us. In classroom matters we likewise often proceed as if the flavor is all. For one example, there is the theory that the best rationale for an addition to the curriculum is to turn a professor loose and let him teach whatever "interests" him. The doctrine that what interests the professors is good for the students reflects a profound faith in personality, and it is probably as responsible as the more familiar causes for what we usually call the anarchy of the curriculum. But is the faith tenable? A C. P. Snow character remarks that it is "an error to think that eminent scholars are very likely to be clever men." Might one risk a charge of unprofessorial conduct and suggest by extension that eminent scholarship does not always imply a concern with central intellectual matters?

But the personality syndrome is really stronger in the outlining of individual courses. I am touched by the unusual condition of a friend —I use the word *condition* in almost the clinical sense—who confessed to me that he hated to teach any course not organized on historical lines because the selection of material placed too much responsibility on his own taste. Alas, poor eccentric, he does not know that flavoring to taste is a professionally acceptable way of molding a course; he has not outgrown a preromantic sensibility that would model a course only on materials that have, or seem to have, objective status. What is more, my lonely friend who is diffident about his taste does not know that history itself often surrenders to the personality of the historian, who is indeed quite willing to invoke his own personality.

To cases. If a professor of the seventeenth century or nineteenth century refuses to teach any of the prose of the period on the ground that he is simply not interested in it, who can gainsay him? Who really believes in the theoretical position he would have to espouse in order to cast the first stone? Another case. A man teaching a historical genre course refuses to include several figures usually considered major or near-major. Professor I (the Inquirer) asks why he does this. Professor HP (the Historian with a Personality) roundly declares that the figures aren't worth teaching. Professor PR (for Principle—an oddball type) says that the omission of these figures means a serious gap in the students' training. Whereupon Professor HP retorts that Professor PR is arrogant, intolerably so, in saying what material Professor HP's course should include. (Professor HP calls it "my course"—that telltale phrase that comes so easily into the professorial mouth and that reverses the movement of recent history, taking us away from the idea of the great

53

communal enterprise and back to a system of private property. Thus we who so often are Democrats in the voting booth reveal a strenuous Republicanism of heart.) Is it not certain that almost any committee on professional practices that you could assemble would vote to sustain Professor HP? No one shall dictate what he is to be interested in, or challenge officially the canon of worthwhile figures created by his personality. If he is giving a course in the history of criticism and limits his study of classical critics to, say, Longinus, can you not hear a colleague, almost any colleague, saying, "Well, I wouldn't do it that way. But it's his point of view, and he's entitled to it. And he does get them excited." Excitement is, I take it, the square or the cube of interest.

Now suppose that Professor HP (this is still our historian with a personality) is teaching the first half of a course of which the second half is being taught by Professor PR (this is still the principle man trying to do without his personality). This is survey of English literature to 1600, and HP has little enthusiasm for earlier figures; so he finds himself arriving at Shakespeare surprisingly quickly, settling there for a long stay, and not managing to stick quite on the offside of 1600 (he has a great interest in tragedy). PR, who takes it up at 1600, finds his class singularly hazy on epic, romance, ballad, allegory, mystery and morality plays, the Petrarchan tradition, and sonnet forms. He complains. But if he is a wise man, he complains only privately; for he knows that if he complained to a committee, the committee would have to say, "Well, if that's what HP wants to do, what can we do, etc., etc.?" But all is not yet lost, for there is one other article in the cult of autonomous personality that might be applied here. Suppose HP, who models a course on his own interests, also models so much of the rest of his life on his own interests that he keeps perpetually colliding with the interests of his colleagues. He is a scourge of the corridors, making colleagues defend their medical practices, their choice of cars, their reading; he doesn't return library books that others need; he harangues others in their offices and makes exorbitantly long calls at their homes. In this situation it might just be possible to have the community take action that would unshakespeare that survey course and restore it to its survey function.

I have heard of a case in which an instructor, assigned to a course in American prose, told the class on the first day that they would spend all their time on American poetry, because in his opinion American prose wasn't worth attention. Now here was a difficult case. But according to my informant, this personalist had fortunately contributed to the easement of the situation by an unfortunate slip: he had already let it be publicly known what he thought of the personalities of his colleagues. He had accused them of being an uninteresting lot. Hence these colleagues found it possible to get the course back into the prosy catalogued groove that the instructor had declared uninteresting. But I find myself thinking: suppose he had been a charm-school boy!

A final example. Most of us, I suspect, have been through the harrowing committee experience of trying to agree on the mandatory contents of a multiple-section course. The unspoken assumption that wisdom flowers where our undammed personalities flow usually impales the committee on a great divide whence tastes and interests splash off east and west—and in many other directions. It is tough log-rolling on these tall slopes of passion. But after the course has been in some way constituted, and by-laws are fought out, the individual participant is quite likely to feel that through some mysterious exemption the rules are not really binding on him. To enforce them would be a form of tyranny, and in the nature of things it is clearly better that the pattern be broken than that his personality be bruised. Even in freshman English the cult of personality is making deviationism a standardized line which only dullards deviate from. My timid friend who hesitated to shape a course on his own taste was distressed to find, on being assigned to a section of freshman literature at his school, that even the syllabus had been ruled out because so many instructors had frowned on it as an oppressive measure, and that he was compelled willy-nilly to steer by inner gleam. If I may be permitted a personal note from my everyday life as a harmless drudge—as an epistolographer, that is— I find that many applicants for positions want to know how we are doing on the personal-freedom front. I think what follows is a fair paradigm of the question that applicants often ask: "How much pressure will I be under in my sections of large courses to conform to prescribed contents and method?" The notable words are *pressure, my, conform*, and *prescribed*. Fearful of being unable to hire anybody except a grammarian or a yes-man who will corrupt our elder statesmen according to Lord Acton's law, I hasten to promise that we will make every effort to keep our anarchy level as high as that at Berkeley, Madison, and other centers of resistance to oppression.

Though I have of course cited some extreme cases, they are, I hope, accurate symbolically; they are the more visible forms of the rather widely diffused cult of interest and interestingness. It is a quirk of history that this cult has grown at the same time that the "mask" has become almost a cliché of literary criticism, and the modes of self-concealment have been especially well understood among the stratagems of the artist. It is ironic that just when everybody has learned that a persona is a mask, almost nobody would think of personality as a state of being masked. Personality, on the contrary, implies a spiritu-

55

al nudism which will be full of fun for all; to drape all these charms with requirements of an impersonal order would be to put virtue in a straitjacket. Though the writer masks his partisanship for the sake of art, the pedagogue's passions are revealed lest his art lack luster.

In certain classroom phenomena we find the instructional principle of passion revealed. The doctrine of interest often leads us to suppose that a class meeting has been especially praiseworthy if it has been marked by dispute and contention. The hour is said to have been interesting, the students are said to have been interested, and this we assume to indicate expanding knowledge and sharpening judgment. A heretic might inquire whether excitement has not been mistaken for enlightment, and the shooting sparks of friction for the less glamorous light of understanding; whether the mind seeking illumination is not simply confused by the pyrotechnics of personality displays; whether the lucid inspection of truth is not lost in the fiery defense of feelings and interests. For there is a complex interrelationship of interest and interests, of personality and property.

The cult of personality not only influences classroom style and tone generally, showering down from above and bubbling up from below, but appears in a special relationship of classroom origin—that of prophet and disciples. It may function also where there is a prophet and no disciples. Whether the leader floats on the shoulders of his flock or has to walk alone, we might first assume that what is involved is the rational cogency of systems of thought. One system lacks philosophic strength, another has it. Nor is this assumption entirely in error. But in our climate a school of thought, whether crowded or empty, has also to be understood in terms of what we may call its personality index. However profound a prophet may be, the prospective follower has the right to be interested or not, and the prophet may be found interesting or not (if he is not, the potential disciple tells him sharply, "Go to heaven," and runs off toward more populous quarters). But this needs to be put a little more precisely. The system of thought which is the formal bond among prophet and disciples, the body of principles assented to and proclaimed, is often less an ordering of ideas than a complex medley of thought and feeling, less a pure construction by the mind than a partly rationalized overflow of powerful personality. This, in turn, while it evokes certain motions of the intellect, becomes effective by engaging the personalities of students; need responds to need; indeed, it is sometimes possible to identify a philosophic school as a collection of individuals united by personality type. A friend of mine, sensitive to this issue, once remarked to me that he was distressed by certain followers of his who were there because he had unwittingly appealed to certain prejudices of theirs—a rare instance of a desire to distinguish among the flow of personality, the stream of consciousness, and the controlled irrigation-system of thought. My friend shied from the untutored response of the autonomous personality; he was unwilling to trust nature, and not labor to convince.

But if a prophet's power lies not only in the bond of thought but also in the nexus of personality, this, we must admit, is not necessarily deplorable. What I am calling personality, though on the one hand it may mean merely an easy appeal to adolescent feeling, and too often does, may in some faculty members, if not as many as one could wish, be deepened and matured by experience, self-criticism, and discipline and may thus mean a wisdom of perception and feeling that of itself may aid the growth of the follower's mind. Or to restate this in different terms: if personality is simply the general force of temperament and disposition, then its value depends on the kind of brains and moral sense it is attached to. But it is just this consideration that is most likely to be forgotten when the cult of personality is powerful.

One final point under the classroom rubric. Suppose we offer a course in something because we are interested in it, and students refuse to be interested in what we are interested in. We are all familiar with the sad picture of the student waiting to be interested by something or even, perhaps defiantly, challenging the professor to interest him. We take a rather dim view of him; he seems not to have aged properly. But I submit that this unenticeable youth is in our own image. He is rudely betraying us by invoking our own doctrine of autonomous interest, and he is putting us into a very pretty dilemma. Our theory provides us no way of both dealing with him and holding on to our own values. We can let him persist in uninterestedness and thus save our principle at the expense of our course. Or we can demand that he be interested and thus save our course at the expense of our principle. For once we admit that interest is a secondary or tertiary value and acknowledge that there are matters which *ought* to claim the attention of human beings, we have unfortunately undermined the defense of the autonomous personality, even our own.

A certain kind of personalitarian has another way out: he can insist that what *he* is interested in is truly basic, and that other personalities can but profit from exposure to his interest. It is an imaginable position, at least to the extent that for all of us the personal faith, the personal concern, tends to acquire an aura of suprapersonal truth. The man for whom this impression becomes conviction and who for the sake of truth will let his own taste become prescriptive exemplifies a certain kind of personalitarian—the dogmatic or monarchic type; he is to be contrasted with the liberal personalitarian who will let all pursuits be dissolved in a relativistic sea of undistinguishable personalities. The true monarchic personalitarian tends to regard the special interests of others as eccentricities, somehow reprehensible, and even in need of corrective action. Have you not heard, let us say, the devotee of the social and political novel take off on a colleague with a taste for comedy of manners? "Why, the man actually admires Trollope. This shows that he's a fraud. He should be disbarred." So the doctrine of personality tends to push us at the same time toward dictatorship and toward an ungovernable pluralistic flux.

The personalitarian sentiment breaks out in odd ways. For years I have been struck by the vehemence with which some humanists scorn or denounce the hundred Great Books; their unforgiving severity has always appeared to exceed somewhat the punishable shortcomings of that hopeful catalogue. In fact I have once or twice had the vague suspicion that insofar as the list might become more convincing, its critics would become the more ireful and polemical. But this supposition remained hazy until one day at a regional meeting, when a friend from another university suddenly came up with a Patrick Henry glint in his eye, and began to abuse the Five-foot Bookshelf. He called it, if I remember correctly, a fraud upon humanity. Though I was a little surprised at this furious beating of a dead bookcase, I saw all at once what was up: this was one man's special version of the attack on the hundred books. The trouble with the five score books and the five feet of shelving was not that they were incomplete, or imperfectly designed, or shoddily executed: it was the idea which they represented. This idea is an affront to the cult of personality, an attack on the individual's sacred right not to be interested. For the unbearable idea is that certain works of the human mind are of such fundamental importance that they demand the attention of the intelligent grownup. And if there are such works with a prescriptive right, gone is the autonomy of the personality; it must yield to something greater than itself. To escape the frivolity of ignoring a valid claim, the cultist must attack such lists, the five score and the five feet, as the creation of error and ignorance, a sovietization of knowledge born of a grievous megalomania. He does.

Hence the patron of a library is far less likely to ask for a list of books of some established claim to attention than he is to ask for a reading list that he would doubtless call "personalized." Imagine the shock of a librarian if a customer asked, not "What would I like?" but "What should I like?" This autonomy of the personality appears even in those pathetic efforts to subdue the inanimate world by the device of "personalized" stationery, handkerchiefs, underwear, etc.: machine-
58

work given the breath of individual life by a monogram. One thinks of personalized checks, too. Unhappily the only truly personalized check is the one that bounces, for it alone escapes into freedom from the rigid impersonal world of checks and balances that denies all scope to personal whim, however interesting the person may be.

Several different hypothetical critics might assess this exaltation of personality in different ways. One critic might argue that within the ivied walls the worship of personality displaces the judging of talent, for when interest is an accepted criterion for choices and decisions, the issue of excellence is bypassed or begged. A sociologist, however, might treat the glorification of personality as simply a phenomenon of the age of automation and masses—a countermovement created by an individuality urgently seeking to be preserved. If the sociologist went on to become a moralist, he might approve the phenomenon as a noble index of the persisting spirit of individual liberty. Another kind of moralist might find the cult of personality to be only an expression of human wilfulness, a new dress for the egotism which formally we know we must shun, but so unrevealing, indeed so flattering, a dress that it makes us forget the customary penalties for self-adulation.

Which of these critiques, if any, contains more than a half-truth I must leave to others to decide. And it is purely in the spirit of the information officer that I recall the injunction laid upon the title-hero of Hermann Hesse's *Steppenwolf* when he was about to be given a number of theatrical views of reality: he was told that, if he was to see truly, he must first free himself from the prison of his personality.

Now for a final word on my initial subject: the eternal destiny of the most interesting people, a destiny which is the ultimate symbol of the cult of interest and personality. Since, as I suggested earlier, even the mildest humanist senses a Faustian infernalist within himself, we can perhaps suitably quote Marlowe's Dr. Faustus on this issue. First there is the early Faustus, as chipper as a professor who has just uttered a blasphemous quip:

> The word *damnation* terrifies not me,
> For I confound hell in Elysium:
> My ghost be with the old philosophers!

The early Faustus is the manifest voice of the gayest downhill types: what lies below, he thinks happily, is a perpetual picnic of "good talk," a hotbed of interestingness. This, I repeat, is the early Faustus. Some scenes further on we find the later Faustus, who has come a little closer to the Elysian atmosphere. Now in the light of additional experience he utters only a poignant wish: "O, might I see hell and return again, how happy were I then!" We might say in modern laboratory terms, to which even humanists are addicted, that the early Faustus experimented with a new hypothesis of hell but after further investigations the later Faustus found it necessary to go back to the older theory. But there is another possibility of interpretation: that there is really a link between the two conceptions of hell, and that the early Faustus saw only part of the picture. That is, in deciding later that hell was a better place for a tourist than for a resident (or, in academic argot, that it was a good place to go from), Faustus was not really changing his initial view but was only coming to see the true nature of the Elysian dream. In other words, though in saying that hell and interestingness go together one may intend only to prophesy good times for himself and the other damned, he may inadvertently reveal a much deeper connection, and a less reassuring one, between the two. And that deeper connection would perhaps be this: that the autonomy of interest and the autonomy of personality—doctrines which overlap enough to be almost identical—are nothing more than forms of that self-indulgence at the heart of all the unhappy deeds for which men are—or once were—sent below.

6

Teaching Careers
and Graduate Schools

Programs and Postures

One of the costs of living in a revolutionary period is the constant outbreaks of all kinds of virtue. Nettling as I find such moral knowingness, with its recipes for the elimination of old vice, and its educational miracle drugs which I suspect will have frightening side effects that no one foresees, I acknowledge that I too will shortly burst into virtue and prescription. Still I am a little put off by one-half of the early 1970s virtue, the half which attaches to the proposition that we should give up pedantry and at long last undertake instruction. The assumption is that heretofore we have taught only research and created a nation of researchers; we will now teach teaching and create a nation of teachers. But I doubt that we have actually taught research or can teach teaching. I am suspicious of the cliché forms of sin and salvation.

On the one hand, the research business has had a somewhat modester role than one would guess from the outbursts of soul on the pedagogical side. Even in my day in graduate school a fair number of people ducked research-oriented seminars because the subjects seemed trifling. More recently I have read a good many graduate students' confidential evaluations of the instruction they have received, and the most consistent theme in these is discontent with seminars, especially with listening to their friends' research reports. Once these new trainees in research get out of graduate school, a surprisingly small percentage publicly practice the activities that we call research. And of that small percentage, only a fraction do it well. I have heard various editors of journals cry out in anguish over the triviality of submissions, and, worse than that, over the badness of the writing.

The first cliché to be shunned, then, is that research has run the show. The second cliché is the meretricious dualism, parroted year

61

after year in and out of the profession, that puts researchers into one bin and good teachers into another. In the only place where such a comparison is relevant—that is, the university where the double life is the way of life—the good man tends to be good in both, and joint excellence is the overwhelming rule; the exceptions stand out sharply just because they are exceptions. Reduced training in research, absence of publication, or deplorable publication cannot be considered automatic sources of good teaching. Conversely, research-oriented training cannot be thought of itself to produce bad teaching. Since entering college in 1923 I have never ceased hearing reports of fine teachers, far more than of bad ones; evil reports have rarely been of revolutionary intensity. In my opinion, the general level of college and university teaching has been far higher than it would appear from the rather chic abuse of it. Good teachers, I suspect, are born rather than made; probably, like football players, they are born in a certain ratio to one hundred thousand of population. I suspect that with adequate imagination and conscience, the potential good teachers become actual, whatever their training stresses, and that if they are short on imagination and conscience, training won't help much.

Just to clear the ground of misconceptions and clichés, I have suggested that if graduate schools reduce the traditional emphasis on research, this will neither endanger scholarship nor guarantee better teaching; that good scholarship has tended to be accompanied by good teaching; that the absence of scholarly publication, or the presence of second-rate scholarly publication, does not guarantee good teaching any more than bad teaching guarantees good scholarship, though an occasional foolish man may have equated them; that teaching on the whole has been better than some critics are pleased to admit; and that given the ordinary frailties of human character and talent, shifting our instructional emphasis to instructional methods will not much enlarge the number of candidates for great-teaching awards. If we keep such points in mind, we may, in considering some new objectives in graduate school, avoid false equations, utopian expectations, and perhaps even evangelistic hubris.

Certain professional facts emerged about 1970 and will continue to trouble us for quite a while. We make peripheral adjustments, true, but behind them lie basic issues that occasion much disagreement. It is these basic issues that I am concerned with, though I approach them in terms of the crisis that brought them to the surface.

Our teaching supply for four-year institutions, we found, exceeds demand. For a long time, however, an enormous amount of teaching is going to be done in two-year colleges. What do we in the graduate schools do about this dual situation? One choice is morally obligatory: when there is a population explosion, the graduate schools have to cut the birth rate of college teachers. Contraception is called for, even though taking the pill may be bitter when expansion is often equated with virtue. (We can't really do much with abortion despite its present popularity; that is, mechanically terminating the academic life conceived when alma mater is entered by a graduate student.) Aside from this obligatory negative step—perhaps the better figure for it would be abstinence, or since it reflects a historical cycle, the rhythm method—what do we do affirmatively? Here we can consider planned parenthood of a different kind of offspring; perhaps even artificial insemination.

The new offspring will not come out of the nowhere into the here; they can come either from the present population of high-school teachers or from those who before the present contraction might have been four-year college teachers. Here it's essential that we do not fall into either of two objectionable attitudes. In one we say to the high-school teacher: "Look, I have good news for you, you're going up in the world; just take this little old special degree we got for you, and we're gonna let you up into a little old junior college." In the other we say to the prospective Ph.D.: "Look, I've got good news for you. In these tight days we've got a job for you in a junior college, and as a double premium we're going to make the graduate-school grind twice as easy as it was before." There will be good candidates in both camps, and while we cannot deny economic facts, we will do well to avoid an air of special profits, consolation prizes, come-on bargains—anything that could suggest a façade of flattery masking a structure of condescension.

There has been much talk of an alternative degree, and there has been much effort to promote a doctor of arts or some other "non-research" degree. I have never been able to get excited about what degree we give, and I have not objected to our inventing an additional route to the Ph.D., since we already have multiple approaches to that ubiquitous laurel. Clearly I have not shared some good people's passion to "save the Ph.D.," and I hope this is not treason *to* the clerks. I'm less concerned about what the degree is than what it represents; in this I see two aspects which I call "program" and "posture." The former is intellectual, the latter moral. Let us take them in order of rising difficulty.

As for program, there is room for much difference of opinion; I will limit myself to several generalities, and acknowledge my prejudices. The central fact about two-year college teaching—and for that matter, a good deal of four-year college teaching—is the need to teach compo-
63

sition and to teach a wide range of literature. In some quarters it is apparently felt, then, that for the teaching of research method we ought to substitute the teaching of teaching method. I shudder at the latter part of this. I have more faith in the communication of a kind of decency of style and of being, of literacy and humanity, from instructors who have these, than I have in the inculcation of pedagogical mechanisms by pedagogical technicians. It is likely that in graduate school we need to work harder at providing models of both writing and teaching instead of planning courses in instructional expertise. Note that this substitutes posture for program, and I need not insist that that is the harder way to do it. To propose it may be naive.

Now, in matters which are clearly in the realm of program, it is obvious that we can get rid of most or all research seminars. But from this regimen I would save one exercise for the professional teacher: I would want him to have one experience in doing a critical bibliography. It is a good discipline in trying to deal with diversity of opinion, in learning that there is diversity of opinion, and in reducing the not infrequent illusion that one's views are fresh and new.

But for the center of graduate instruction for teachers who will have to teach diverse fields, I can think of no more intrinsically useful and thoroughly delightful graduate regimen than one based on the widest possible reading of primary literary documents—plays, poems, fiction, essays, criticism. On the useful side it will be a hedge against two kinds of creeping provincialism that threaten the ecumenism natural to literary studies. One kind is inherent in the old scholarship: scholarship means specialization, specializing means knowing a field totally, this means knowing others very little if at all, and pretty soon you have a man boasting about his ignorance in other fields because this ignorance seems to prove his genius in his own and, conversely, abusing as a dilettante anyone who is crass enough to know something of a field other than his own. But a still worse parochialism is that of many students who want to study only what they already know or like; they need protection against an assumed right to ignorance, or against remaining midgets when they could achieve full growth. Aside from this usefulness, think of the sheer delightfulness of reading as widely as possible in works of imagination. I feel very dogmatic about this; if a student does not experience delight in reading in many types and fields, he ought to be in some other profession.

(This is as good a place as any to declare that if the field of English is ever destroyed, it will be destroyed, not by scientists and social scientists, but by people in English who don't like literature. They have got into the field because some very small segment of it happened to gratify their emotions at some critical period, and they have thence on proclaimed that they don't need to know anything but that. The creeping ignorance which threatens the field through the self-interest of intellectually and emotionally undisciplined individuals is a greater danger, I think, than has been realized.)

If the most extensive possible reading is, as I believe, a superb graduate regimen for teachers, then how organize the reading? I think one needs a primary mechanical ordering, and a secondary intellectual ordering; hence I would stick to basic historical patterns, with the strongest possible overlay of the nonhistorical, such as diverse critical methods. Knowing chronology and periods is helpful in reducing general chaos and the specific provincialism in time that afflicts each new modernity. Knowing various critical approaches means having diverse ways into the nonhistorical essence which I take to be the final object of our search. With an awareness of the complex interplay of the historical and the nonhistorical in imaginative writing, the wide-ranging, flexible generalist, at home on several axes, is most likely to provide the model of broad knowledge and of concern plus detachment that should contribute to pedagogical effectiveness.

Obviously I believe more in literacy, in quantity of knowledge, and in variety of perspective than I believe in how-to courses, and I believe more in our modeling excellence than in our explicating it. So what I have called program and posture are constantly intertwined. There is one matter, however, that has to do with posture alone, and it is the most important of all. The problem is a moral one, and it is the same in teaching as in driving a car: what we need is a sense of obligation rather than a sense of privilege. I'm not giving a fight-talk for what used to be called selflessness; I just want better patterns of self-approval. In brief we need to love ourselves for doing something that needs doing rather than for shoving it off on someone else. Our egos will always stay with us, but we can train ourselves to gratify them by heeding imperatives rather than by claiming exemptions, by getting with it rather than getting away with it. But our graduate schools have almost unconsciously conditioned their products to anticipate privileges rather than feel obligations; we all share in the responsibility for this, and we need to do a little moral homework.

The central obligation that needs to be felt is the obligation to teach whoever is there to teach. Some people regard teaching as only a subsistence operation that makes it possible to devote prime time and energy to something else, or themselves as volunteers who can expect to operate only very selectively. One young colleague, objecting to teaching a sophomore course, said to me, "I shouldn't be used in this way; I am a scholar." There is a quite widespread expectation, perhaps

unconscious, that the profession should serve the individual by gratifying his preconception of himself. Here I must again mention the job
applicant who writes me, after two years as a teaching assistant, "I
think I have done my time in freshman English." This is the negative
version of sense of privilege. It appears affirmatively in the expectation
that the department will produce seminars for one as soon as possible.
A special form of this is the inquiry: "How do you expect me to write
if you don't give me a seminar?" Here the expected privilege is that of
having other people dig up the stuff to be funneled into one's publication machinery. Or the motive may be as a bright skeptical colleague
of mine puts it: "Oh, seminars are lazy work. The instructor doesn't
do anything, so he loves it. He just sits there and listens and says,
'Well, well.'" At least this is consistent with graduate students' ac-
counts of seminars. Then there is the kind of job applicant of whom
his referees say, "He is more successful with superior students." The
kind of teacher who can cut it only with valedictorians embodies another kind of self-indulgence: a freedom from having to work at
communicating with the large body of students there to be taught.

Lest this seem like crabbed age venting its spleen on golden boys
and girls, let me enter two disclaimers. The first is that the best professional conscience I have seen is in a young man who is as devoted a
teacher as he is a lively, erudite, and productive critic. He has done
two things. One, he has constantly requested teaching assignments in
junior-division courses and pure composition courses because he has
felt that that is where the big instructional job is really most needed.
Two, he has urged his colleagues to deploy their best teaching strength
in junior-division courses, on the ground that *that* is where the most
teaching is to be done, since upper-division people and graduate students largely teach themselves. This is a splendid counter to the illusion
held by some of us that great faculty minds can speak only to great
student minds and that therefore, if one can reach few students, one
must be very profound. I have never heard a faculty member say, "I
have not a great mind and prefer to deal with less gifted students," or,
"I don't have great thoughts, so anyone can understand me."

My second disclaimer is that, if the expectation of privilege tends to
stand out most dazzlingly in junior colleagues, it is because they are
closer to graduate school; there they learned it from us old boys, and
change has to start with us. This is the central matter of posture, and of
our obligation to provide models that will not beget a mistaken sense
of privilege, exemptions, and special roles. I have never heard of a
graduate school mentor's telling his young followers that the career
ahead is one of tasks requiring commitment, of difficulties requiring
vocation, of needs to be met by devotion and struggling ingenuity. I

have never heard of his telling a new Ph.D., "Go to X college: they badly need your talents." Instead he says things like this: "Don't go there, the winters are terrible"; "Don't go there, the president is an engineer"; "Don't go there, they have no graduate students"; "Don't go there, the local symphony is no good"; "Don't go there, I never heard of anyone there"; "Don't go there, the town isn't liberal"; "Don't go there, the library isn't aircooled"; "Don't go there, the wind blows a lot"; "Don't go there, it's south of the Mason and Dixon line (isn't it?)"; in a word, "Don't go there, the human beings there aren't as human as you are." All this disesteem is of course a form of self-esteem; our own place is first rate, we know, but we are more sure of it if we can keep assigning defects to other places.

Hence there is something a little ironic in the joint MLA-ADE advisory, issued in September of 1970 to departments with new Ph.D.'s to move: encourage them to take a reasonable view of possibilities. The principle is fine, of course; but it won't work if all that *we* have said—and *done*—has encouraged a dreamy or escapist view of reality, if we have directly or implicitly treated professional life as an elitist Eden with only few classes and choice or few or no students. My point is that we need, by showing it in action, to create a sense of obligation rather than privilege, a concern for doing what has to be done rather than for getting out of or away with something. Any man will avoid excessive expectations if he learns by example to expect to respond to a need, or better, by needing to respond to a need.

Finally we must further—this by our own style in teaching—another obligation, the obligation to teach the field instead of oneself. We cannot say with Sidney, "Look in thy heart and teach." (Here I turn to another phase of the subject discussed at length in "The Cult of Personality.") One of my most depressing moments as chairman was when a junior colleague told me that we should revamp our curriculum, particularly by inventing a lot of new courses that would reflect the "personal interests" of the faculty. This reduction of the field to an extension of the personality, or of the individual work to a projection of the instructor's sensibility—this destroys the field and the works. It is another substitution of privilege for obligation, the obligation to comprehend and present the field or work as objectively as we can. In this we know that we will not succeed wholly; but if we are aware of subjectivity and will try to discipline it, we will at least escape the radical subjectivity which erodes away the field. If in self-love we as teachers simply communicate ourselves to students, we do them the great disservice of depriving them of that larger reality which we ourselves do not approximate, and of encouraging crotchetiness. At most we

67

lead them from their privacy into our privacy, which is a somewhat questionable gain. The students from eighteen to twenty are in great need of having opened for them the largest world that literature can open; they present a large opportunity to furnish ways out of the little cell of self which we all have to grow out of. Their instructors will do this if by our example in graduate school we communicate to them with the right posture, if as their teachers we stay in the largest possible public domain and thus encourage what I have called the obligation to teach the subject instead of oneself.

I am violating rules of composition by being very general. But so many people have been making specific curricular proposals for a new graduate regimen that I saw no point in getting into that game. I have proposed only one broad program: get students to read all the literature they can—for the pleasure of it, for the tempering of the parochial, for the expansion of mind and spirit. Let the instructor be the voice of the large world rather than of the small area or the small self. Perhaps wrongly, I do not have much faith in ad hoc pedagogical devices, in novel classroom mechanisms, in how-to courses, in the teaching of teaching generally or in the teaching of the teaching of composition. At most such operations would be ancillary and peripheral. I fear our settling on technical or methodological substitutes for the achieving of right qualities of mind and attitude—that is, seeking curricular answers to moral problems, particularly now when we have an exacerbated sense of the outmoded, and when all innovation seems salutary. We should, in other words, not confuse program and posture. It is easier to invent courses than to alter professional style. But perhaps the most significant thing we can do in graduate school is change a style that is not very helpful to the teaching career, in two-year—or for that matter four-year—colleges. At the center of this style is the assumption that it is better to be a specialist than a generalist, that the profession owes us privileges rather than that we have obligations to it, that it is desirable to be where there is least call upon our instructional talents rather than the most, that we ought to do what we want to do rather than want to do what ought to be done. Beneath all of these assumptions lies a need to think well of oneself. In no sense do I urge that we think ill of ourselves or not think of ourselves. Good man and bad man alike will continue to think of self. But the best thing the good man can do is find better ways to think well of himself.

AT LECTERN, TYPEWRITER, AND CONFERENCE TABLE:
A PROBLEM OF STYLE

7
Freedom
from Speech
Vigilance Revisited

In virtually every decade of my adult life, it seems to me, some public event or other has led to a new outbreak of anguished cries on behalf of freedom of speech and against forces or persons supposed to be threatening that freedom. This eternal vigilance is a necessity, as we hardly need to be told again. On the other hand, our vigilance might well include the sense that the very act of calling for freedom of speech can bear a little inspection too. One man, who could be a professor as well as a man in the street, may call for freedom of speech to cloak his need to shock or wound others. Another man may call for freedom of speech in order to gain or retain the power to take away other men's freedom. A newspaper may call for freedom of speech to protect its revenues or its sense of power. Such cases account for a certain undercurrent of discomfort that I often feel when verbal vigilance becomes too audible. Many kinds of the speech that we want freedom for do not lead to freedom. We might ask, then, "Freedom of what speech?"

Instead, however, I want to proclaim a necessary counterfreedom, freedom *from* speech. I hasten to say that I am proposing, not universal vows of silence or the elimination of political campaigns, but a more taxing kind of vigilance than that which we usually practice. I mean, in short, freedom from messy speaking, freedom from the worst of all speech habits, freedom from what often passes for speech but actually is no more than familiar sounds that defraud us by pretending to communicate facts and truths. We may call this, more precisely, freedom from clichés—the con men of the realm of words. Freedom from clichés means both a sharp eye for the words of others and the agonizing reappraisal of one's own vocabulary to eliminate slogans, catchwords, wastebasket terms—all the well-worn phrases that give the

71

illusion of thought while actually interfering with thought. I am speaking for that virtue of mind of which the outward sign is precision of speech: freedom from words plus power over words.

There are three basic kinds of imprecision which I will figuratively call highbrow, middlebrow, and lowbrow. Highbrow imprecision is pretentious: the user of words is seduced by multitude of syllables or novelty of sound. When a scholar wants to talk about his method but uses the word *methodology,* which means something quite different, he reveals a virgin mind seduced by three extra syllables. When he means *reverse* but says *obverse,* which means the reverse of reverse, he is evidently so fascinated by the more exotic sound that he doesn't mind saying the reverse of what he means. Sometimes he says *interpersonal* when he means *personal.* At the opposite extreme is lowbrow imprecision, the product of a blundering eye and ear. When a student or a professor means *militate* against but says *mitigate* against, this is not an affectation founded on ignorance, but unaffected ignorance itself. Our present business lies not with these extremes but with middlebrow or bourgeois imprecision. This is the great empire of the cliché, in which words become loose symbols of attitudes rather than tight delineators of thought, and in which the easy repetition of words that denote vague, standardized current feelings and postures persuades the user that he is engaging in mental activity. Clichés are the unredeemable scrip of a white-collar class living on intellectual credit.

Liberty requires not only a watchfulness against encroachments from without but also a resistance against temptations from within. These are two complementary tasks, neither of which may be quite easy: freedom from others, and freedom from oneself. On the one hand, one is trying to keep certain characters from setting up concentration camps; on the other, one tries to keep oneself from rushing into these camps to reserve rooms. I can understand many actions of men only by means of this postulate: that we have as strong an instinct to be slaves as we have desire to be free. I am profoundly convinced that we deceive ourselves if we believe that we love only liberty. (There is in the world, of course, a truly great love of wilfulness, which, in trying to make itself socially presentable—to keep its slips from showing—presents itself as a passion for freedom. The outbreaks of wilfulness are among the prices we pay for a libertarian atmosphere.)

I suggest this hidden inclination to slavery not to disparage humankind but to try to get that completeness of picture without which we cannot talk sensibly on the subject of freedom. When we hear the word *liberty,* what comes most easily to mind, for all of us, is a delightful contemplation of other people's misdeeds and a vision of

72

pleasurable heroics for ourselves. Now, however, I am proposing, not crusades and brinkmanship, but only a mild domestic-aid program—a modest, unspectacular, and yet not easy one: not freedom from chains, but freedom from phrases. This offers a minimum of public excitement, and a maximum of private responsibility. Phrases are less like chains than like dope; we cannot gloriously hack our way out of them by sheer muscle and courage while the band plays Sousa, but we have to learn to spot them, to resist their relentless temptations, and perhaps to get over a habit. Anyone who wishes to lead an honorable life of mind may start quietly with precision in words. In this quest one may have to give up at least three kinds of words: Fourth of July words, that is, glorious terms that provide temporary sparkle but no real light; Maginot Line words, that is, self-protective terms that keep out criticism by others or oneself; and guillotine words, those quick slicer terms that behead an enemy and thus keep him from breathing syllables that we don't like to hear. Here is a spot for eternal vigilance— but not vigilance before the footlights or on the front page.

As an example of a cliché term that has a national spread and that can have Fourth of July, Maginot Line, and guillotine functions, let us take the term *Americanism*. This is a term that has no objective meaning, and it is harmful because it arouses nationalistic emotions that blind us to real problems of value; some users of this term even employ it with the very purpose of spreading confusion and darkness. If we want a significant term for political and social excellences that we can all espouse in America, the term must never be a geographical one, since geographical boundaries are not boundaries of good and evil. Any virtues that we can safely claim or aspire to for American life are also open to the possession of all other nations; virtues are not like physical territory that can be possessed by only one country; indeed, all true virtues are not only open to all nations but must be sought out equally by them. The underlying vice of the term *Americanism* is that it implies a regional monopoly of merits that have nothing to do with regions and cannot be thought of in regional terms. To use such a term is a piece of intellectual and moral provincialism, which we would easily spot in our northern and southern neighbors if they kept boasting about supposedly unique achievements under such terms as *Canadianism* and *Mexicanism* and kept ceaselessly shoving these terms down our throats as the names of an exclusive moral excellence. (If we bristle at such terms as *Pan-Arabism, Pan-Asianism,* and *Pan-Africanism,* we should remember that these are the Americanisms of non-American worlds.) In sum the cliché *Americanism* confuses the diverse problems of self-description, self-understanding, and legitimate aspiration;

73

self-esteem with a tenable patriotism, which is critical of imperfections; and a sense of quality with a love of locality.

For the preceding point I have been denounced by a right-wing columnist; the necessary balancing point will doubtless not seem lovable to the left. For what is as bad as, or worse than, the undiscriminating use of *Americanism* is the counterphenomenon for which there is no single word—the savage anti-Americanism that a number of intellectuals (professors and journalists) took up during the 1960s. Whereas the users of *Americanism* spread confusion through innocence, the anti-Americanists spread it through calculation. The former want to save something undefined, the latter want to snatch a well-defined power. They have not a single cliché but a series, such as *system, tyranny*, and *imperialism*. Unlike the users of *Americanism* they know that their sacred terms are nonsense (in the sense that, should their D-Day come, they would use power to practice what they preach against). But through their clichés they hope to beguile those in the middle who have not been, or once were, beguiled by *Americanism*.

We find the same coast-to-coast spread in two other popular clichés—*comfort* and *happiness*. These are not clichés if they are simply used to denote hypothetical states of body and mind which now and then may exist in fact but which are important mainly as a challenge to our powers of definition. They are clichés if they are accepted as terms for values that are supposed to be worthy of serious pursuit. It is just in this dubious sense that *comfort* and *happiness* are favorite terms of American advertising. When such terms are always in the air they tend to be picked up by many people who are capable of being more discerning but who, by using these clichés, increase their own and everybody else's confusion about the ends of life. Once a person escapes from or resists the cliché atmosphere he may identify comfort correctly—that is, as an attribute of the hen roost and the cow barn, and he may recognize happiness as the most seductive mirage that ever led mankind on endless shortcuts over the wide and prickly sands of actuality. Then he may become open to less delusive but almost forgotten terms for desirable states and actions—*sense of reality, obligation*, even *renunciation*. This assumes, of course, that he will not have been trapped by a more recent cliché that translates comfort into quasi-philosophic idiom but does not lessen the folly of the thought—"rejection of the work ethic." Users of this cliché usually add the word "Protestant," not noting that it was pre-Protestant Aristotle who defined happiness as a by-product of working.

A certain suspicion of football in the late 1960s made some headway, I am sure, not because in those tempestuous days we had a new accession of logic or virtue, but because many people who were not

74

antifootball did become a bit weary of the monstrous clichés parroted in defense of it. Football is the most fertile unmarried mother of clichés that modern universities ever gave a foster home to. We all know about the extraordinary achievements for education, character, and society that have been attributed to several months per year of highly specialized exercises by a small minority group of experts in head-knocking. Once we get out from under the shadow of the clichés, we see that football has neither more nor less relationship to, say, character, than a student's job or studies or ordinary relations to others; in all of these, we may practice certain decencies or we may not. We create ourselves by doing or not doing what we ought to do—meeting our kind of assignments or not meeting them, meeting them honestly or slickly, vigorously or casually. A blocker or running back can be as big a rascal as a plagiarist in the library or an exhibitionist in the classroom. Specialized muscles will not automatically save him from dishonesty or meanness or prolonged immaturity.

I happen to like football; I am only arguing for a freedom from falsifying phrases. We can talk about a sport sensibly only if we understand its actual function. I will make one suggestion about the function of football—namely, that what happens to both participants and spectators is a kind of working off of latent savagery. We could put this in Aristotelian terms and call it a catharsis of savagery. If this is a tenable description of what happens, then we at least know where we are. We could proceed from there to a consideration of whether the catharsis of savagery is a justifiable auxiliary function of a place traditionally committed to nourishing the intellect. On this large subject I will do no more than note one con and one pro. The con is that education is already dangerously close to trying to do everything under the sun, and that it might be better not to undertake to purge even a fraction of the id. The pro is that there may be a real gain for wisdom in having, under the very nose of the mind, a reminder of our primitive inheritance; that our service of the intellect might be better managed if we had a sound idea of the whole being of which it is a part. It may even be socially desirable to recognize the id and work some of it off in these ways. Professed revolutionaries always oppose football: whatever of violence and destructiveness it releases they want to grab and turn to their own ends. Dissidents against football, who may or may not be revolutionaries, have now discovered their own cliché: they always call the game "dehumanizing"—a pure play for the innocent in the grandstand, who may not stop to reflect that everything that is done in football comes right out of human nature. (There is hope for the language, however, when a city comes up with bumper stickers to to applaud its most vigorous defensive lineman: "Support your local

dehumanizer." Ironic metaphor is one excellent antidote to the cliché.)
Left and right have counterbalancing clichés, as usual: football will
destroy humanity, football will save democracy and the country.

Fancy phrases for plain missions festoon the air not only of the ath-
letic publicity office but also of the faculty club. There are, for instance, the purple words by which teachers often describe their own
work—namely, that they are "training" students to "think for themselves." At the risk of arousing the committee on unprofessorial conduct, I must say that this faculty cliché is on the grand side. I will ignore the case in which we instructors try to teach students to think like
ourselves and speak of it as teaching them to think for themselves. I
will also ignore the case of our distress when a student whom we are
thus teaching to think for himself chooses to think like some colleague
whose thinking we don't like. Quite aside from little slipups of this
sort, "thinking for oneself" is another case of a rather fancy term that,
so far as I know, has never undergone a thorough examination. We
can think pretty well of ourselves if we can think of ourselves as edu-
cating people to "think" in the abstract, without any limit imposed by
our fields or by our own shortcomings. Now, if a man in my field
who thinks of himself as a thinking-trainer really thinks about what he
is doing, this is what he will have to think: he is making available to
students some of the tools which may be used for thinking about materials in the field of English. I say "some of the tools" because few of
us have such capacious minds that we successfully master and demonstrate all of the tools. I say "thinking about materials in the field of
English" because the tools may have little or no use for thinking in
other fields. Granted, the instructor in English (it is his professional
hazard) may have and may air ideas on nonliterary subjects—on the
university administration or civic morality—and some of the students
may then echo him. If he can think of this transfer of attitudes as instruction in the art of thought, he is indeed doing a pretty good job of
thinking big.

Once we have got over these little foibles of self-approval, we must
face the fact that, in any basic sense, thinking for oneself is accomplished only by an infinitesimally small number of human beings—the
few creators of ideas and concepts that provide the patterns for the
world's thought. The great mass of ordinarily intelligent people are
fated to live forever by the perceptions and imaginings of a minority
of great original minds. This is no cause for shame; it is simply the
way things are. What the rest of us *can* do is choose for ourselves
which of the great thinkers will do our thinking for us (*if* we happen
to have learned something about the great thinkers); or at least we can
choose between great thinkers and small thinkers (*if* we happen to

76

have learned about some unfashionable ideas that will help us distinguish among current fashionable ones). This is no small matter. The chief thing is to know that this is what is meant by thinking for ourselves. We are in trouble if we suppose it means making basic intellectual decisions ourselves, coming up with new insights, new criteria of value, innovating ideas, creative affirmations. If we think this, we are in great danger of mistaking mere private feeling for valid public thought. A larger danger of the cliché of thinking for ourselves is that it may suggest that everyone thinks equally well for himself, that is, that there is no superiority of thought. But there is superiority of thought, and the best way of thinking for ourselves is trying to spot that superiority and profit from it. As a small part of this task we can at least examine men's key terms and see whether these are clichés or apparently live carriers of thought.

In looking for definitions, we struggle, also, against what has been called "language pollution." I assume that language pollutants are less the clichés that persist out of thoughtlessness and habit than the slogans designed to produce thoughtlessness and habit, i.e., subservience. We recognize those that come from the government, as we show by coining the term "credibility gap." I doubt whether we do so well on the other side—in recognizing that when the word *workers* is most loudly shouted, it means that the workers are to be used by self-picked leaders; that *people's* (as in "people's party") means that as many people as possible are to be controlled by a very few; that *democracy* means a powerful doctrinaire oligarchy; that *freedom* means being unrestrained in the production of a chaos where all liberty ends.

Such language pollution is of course a planned subversion of intellectual and moral ecology. But the planners are sometimes given unconscious aid by well-meaning finicky people who, though well behaved themselves, get the pip whenever they hear terms denoting order and the legitimate power essential to maintain it. Some years ago, in a conference which I was attending, it came about that one particular word was generally accepted as a key bad word, so that if any view, idea, or theory could be connected with this word, the view, idea, or theory was immediately cast into the furnace of contempt. The word with such powers of inflicting disgrace was the word *authority*, which in many quarters is still a bad word. At no time did any participant in the conference attempt to define this term of abuse —to distinguish between the rude authority of bare power, that is, illegitimate coercion, and the indispensable authority of position legitimately held; between the blunt assertion of will, and the inevitable power that comes from knowledge and integrity; between the dictatorial enunciation of old saws, new thought-controls, and official points of view, and that most intangible and yet most irresistible of all authorities, the authority of experience or of insight or of wisdom. Obviously we were under the authority of a cliché individualism. If we had been really thinking for ourselves in that conference, our first step would have been to examine one of our key terms to find out what an undifferentiated medley of concepts it brought into play—to seek our own freedom from speech.

In describing automatic responses to *authority* I used the word *we*. Now I must take the last regretful step from first person plural to first person singular. For anyone who is playing at being critic, of course, the happiest grammatical spot is the third person plural: when one can identify all wrongs with "they," he can enjoy a fine freedom of attack. If the critic shifts to first person plural, he loses some of the luster of innocence which is a great help in scourging abuses. If he finally speaks in the first person singular, he surrenders all the indignant righteousness of the man who has not sinned. But he has, alas, to take this step, for the best knowledge of wrongdoing, as all grown-up writers know, comes from introspection.

Quite a few years ago I wrote an essay in which I used the word *reason* as a self-evident definition of human excellence; I was defending this faculty against someone who I thought had traduced it. Perhaps a year or two afterwards I wrote another passage in which, in emphasizing some other value, I spoke of purely rational activities disparagingly, noting even how they might be affiliated with vice. Not until some time later did I become aware that I had been inconsistent because I had been using *reason* as a cliché—that is, a ready-made, unanalyzed term, purporting to denote an objective entity, but actually serving to express an attitude (or, for me, two different attitudes). I was oscillating between two different values. I now regard both these values as indispensable and actually as complementary, but at that time I did not clearly place them, that is, find adequate terms for them.

The word *reason* is worth some attention because in academic life it has become a favorite cliché. That is, it is a vague but sonorous term—a pipe organ term—by which we express approval or disapproval, gratify certain emotions, and even escape the pain of accurate thought. As some men use the word *reason,* it becomes a kind of defense of one's own preconceptions, and a weapon against the preconceptions of others, which are always referred to as "prejudices" and "superstitions." In this usage "Be reasonable" means not much more than "See it my way." Oddly enough *reason* is often the favorite value-word of especially temperamental and tempestuous people, even, in several cases I know, of people wildly intemperate, or charmingly illogical, or

78

vexatiously inconsistent, perhaps downright imperceptive on one hand, or subtly intuitive on the other. They characteristically take a dim view of the emotionalities of others but cling tenaciously to their own feelings, apparently bypass the discomforts of self-inspection, and thus remain convinced that their positions and attitudes are those of a self-evident, undeniable reasonableness. But what looks like a joke on them is, in the end, a joke on all of us. For the equating of reason with what we like or what we strive for—be it a petty profit or a noble end—is a cliché of our whole culture. To this practice we may give the name *logolatry*. It is a habit of speech and feeling that has been growing stronger ever since the Enlightenment. When we say, "Be a reasonable man," we often do not mean anything much different from what certain ancestors of ours would have meant in saying, "Be a Christian," or "Be a loyal subject," or "Be a true Roman."

If we want to try to free ourselves from *reason* as a cliché we can try to distinguish the legitimate content of the word from the emotional additives slipped in by the users. Properly, reason denotes certain powers of animate being that transcend the automatic biological activities: the observation and analysis of phenomena, the formulation of principles that govern phenomena, the use of these principles toward human ends; the analysis, application, and reconstitution of concepts. Insofar as doing something that animals cannot do is a virtue in human beings, engaging in these rational activities is a virtue; being rational is a virtue in the sense that it is desirable for human beings to employ all the human faculties and not to be content with those that they share with all animals. If we use *reason* to denote only these distinguishing human powers, we are safe.

But in facing up to cliché usages, we have to observe that being rational—this power that marks men off from animals—is in itself morally neutral. We cannot speak of reason as though it automatically meant or guaranteed good—or for that matter as if it automatically meant or guaranteed evil—for it can mean or lead to either. It can serve any kind of end whatever. It is an agent or instrument—like an automobile, which can take us to a Socratic debate or to an opium den. Hence, when we praise higher education as the training of mind, we would be on safer grounds if we regarded this as a purely technical process, like training the body or training the voice, and felt primarily that it is a good thing to do a technical process well. But we let a large amount of hope slip into our praise; we take it for granted that the development of rational faculties leads to good ends, such as the deepening of knowledge and the betterment of the world. We forget that reason itself simply does not imply good ends. Some of the most energetic reasoners in Shakespeare are his villains—Goneril and Regan, and

79

especially Iago. Some of his very admirable people have almost no power of reason—Cordelia and Desdemona. A great explorer might have reasoned that the Atlantic would lead to the Indies, but reason did not produce the powerful impulses and the monstrous tenacity required to test the hypothesis. It is not reason that tells us that death is preferable to loss of liberty, or that all men are created equal, or that he who would save his life must lose it.

All I am doing here is noting a few reminders that good conduct and good ends and good values may spring from nonrational sources —from mandates whose origin we scarcely know, whether we call them honor or duty or belief; from aspirations that run counter to all common sense; from modes of apprehension that are by no means free of mystery—intuition (or even extrasensory perception), or imagination, or mystical insight. I say this not to disparage reason, through which we secure many possessions that we cherish, and should cherish, deeply. But it is also the producer of ends and meanings that have lost their hold on most of us; no scientist, no philosopher in one of the modern idioms, reasons more sharply than various medieval theologians. And reason may also be the means to ends that we loathe and detest. Our enemies, for instance, seem not at all defective in using brilliant knowledge and great powers of mind for purposes that cause us some anxiety.

I have spent this much time on the cliché use of reason because I believe it is very important to keep this problem in perspective. One does no good to human life, or to that complex virtue which we call "sweet reasonableness," by using the word *reason* as a loose, all-embracing, omnisemantic term for whatever we admire at any given time, or as a cure-all for what is wrong, or as a source of spiritual growth. One can be effectively reasonable only by knowing the limits of reason. This is not a new idea. I have already cited Shakespeare on the subject. Swift shows Gulliver cracking up under the strain of trying to be a 100-percent-pure rational man. Other artists have shown the human tendency to rebound from an excessive rationality into a terrible irrationality. One of the most influential twentieth-century novelists, D. H. Lawrence, preached year after year for a restoration of the instinctual. But since he is a half-truth prophet, I want to enter another disclaimer: just as I do not disparage reason properly used, so I do not offer the slightest encouragement to the professional irrationalists, who damn all reason as a fraud and leap over into the opposite extreme of an undiscriminating instinctivism where a terrifying medley of virtues and vices are massed under a single holy name. One unhappy form of the reaction against logolatry or reason-worship is what we may call biolatry or life-worship. Out at its opposite pole, indeed, *life* is a cliché value-term as fashionable and as harmful as *reason.* The very fight for freedom from the cliché might be conceived of as a positive endeavor to find a truly preserving position somewhere between the two half-truth extremes, the way-out idolatries, that I have denoted by the two terms *logolatry* and *biolatry.*

Freedom from clichés is less a matter of originality of style than of clearness of thought (in a later essay on critics I will point out that, as an antidote to clichés, originality can have its own boobytraps). We will find some useful images for the problem if we remember that a synonym for cliché, the word *trite,* is related to the words *attrition* and *detritus.* In this family of words the central idea involves erosion, wearing down, debris, and rubble. It is a piece of comic irony that, as carriers of our thought, we should often use words so worn down that they should be sent to the junk pile or the reconditioning plant. If we go a step further into the *trite* family of words, we find that they all come from a root which means *rub.* The ultimate image in the word *trite* is an image of something rubbed down to a nubbin, all distinctive form and identity gone. One is reminded of gangster slang, "rub out." We will probably not often refer to a rubbed-out gang victim as a trite man; nor will this unhappy character, unlike a trite word, often be mistaken for alive. However, a dead man may become a live issue, and I am hoping that in a few of our favorite dead words—trite words, rubbed-out words—we may find live issues for our minds.

The beginning of the life of the mind is freedom from clichés. This freedom appears in two ways. In the first place it is freedom from others who may be trying to put something over on us, may be trying to inhibit our thoughtfulness or even diminish our freedom, by bandying popular terms that do not have an examinable meaning. This freedom from others is the more exciting and magnetic kind of freedom. I do not mean to underrate it if I suggest that it is less important than the other way in which freedom from clichés appears—that is, as freedom from ourselves, from our efforts to put something over on ourselves, by arguing or talking in easy, well-rubbed phrases that represent hackneyed thought or no thought at all. Pursuing this kind of freedom is taxing; it is unspectacular, for there are no grandstands of beneficiaries cheering on their favorite watchdog; instead it belongs to the very private realm of quiet homework. There are no conventional public rewards: the citizen who escapes from the bonds of clichés will not get a medal for bravery or an honorary degree; he will not be celebrated in textbooks as a man ahead of his time, or be chosen his city's man of the year. But he *will* have rewards: he will have the sense of not having fooled himself; and, above all, the rare,

81

exciting inner pleasure of knowing, now and then, that he has had a new understanding and is at least a little more clearheaded than he was before. This is one of the pleasures of the civilized man. And here pleasure and profit are combined, since freedom from speech is the first step in freedom of speech.

8
Verbal Traffic and Moral Freight

Gown and Town

Here again I am in the general realm of the cliché, or at least of often-used words in which more is present than meets the eye. In "Freedom from Speech" my main theme was a verbal currency that we pick up and use to praise or blame, to denote ends to be sought or shunned, without thinking through the implications; thus we give up a freedom that ought to be ours. In one of the terms mentioned, however, we saw another element: an implied grandeur by which the user confers a certain glory upon himself. This was the teacher's definition of his function as "teaching people to think." This kind of thing is worth a further look. My present theme, then, is the way in which we use words to please ourselves, to let ourselves feel a warm inner glow. We appear to be stating only a fact or a truth, but we are really showing that we are on the right side of something. In this practice we aren't lying; without thinking, we are only doing what gratifies us.

Take the phrase "people who care." We may mean ourselves or others; in either case we point with pride. We forget that the phrase does not mean anything at all. It cannot and never will mean anything unless it is followed by a phrase beginning with the word *for*. There are no people who care in the abstract; people can care only for something that is specified, be it public transportation, miniskirts, pure air, game preservation, or deodorants. "Caring" does not, as some of us may think, establish moral superiority. There are those who care a great deal for fornication, strange habits, shots in the arm, and destruction. We forget them. It is exactly the same with the phrase "people who are concerned" or "concerned faculty members." There is no such thing as concerned people. Hence there are two advantages for those who present themselves as concerned. They can think of themselves as having some sort of civic virtue, or even moral elevation, without having proved anything at all. What is far worse, the phrase can be used by partisans with definite objectives in view to delude others into thinking that they are truly public-spirited characters. I am never more concerned than when I find some faculty outfit calling itself "concerned." To see what they are up to, I have to work twice as hard as if they had just said, "We the undersigned support," etc.

But nefariousness is not my subject. I'm thinking rather of something that most of us do at some time or other: use words that make us feel good inside because they put us on the right side and let us expect cheers from the outside. By "verbal traffic" I mean those busy words that we use a good deal because they contain some gratification for us. By "moral freight" I mean those aspects of the meaning that we don't pay attention to, not because we are dishonest but because we are human and love ourselves. We forget how easy it is to use approvingly such words as *democracy, integration,* and *peace* and thus to exhibit piety and rectitude. We forget how hard it is to use such words neutrally, to base a cool discussion on them, and to face up to the enormous complications in subjects opened up by the words. In our usage there is a hidden profit motive—maybe that of ease, maybe that of subtle self-esteem, maybe that of the quest for approval. Or, to repeat the figure in my title, verbal traffic may carry a hidden freight, and we need a semantic customs inspection to see whether any intellectual or moral bootlegging is going on.

Take that ringing phrase which made so many users of it feel good during the 1960s—"Tell it like it is." All it seems to say is, "Tell the truth." But look at all the moral cargo—all the hidden implications so heart-warming to the speaker: (1) I alone am a good guy interested in truth; (2) the world is full of bad guys trying to conceal the truth; (3) most people have not known the truth or have not wanted to know it; (4) it will hurt them to know the truth, and that will be good for them; (5) the truth will mean showing up a lot of shady people who have bamboozled or injured us; (6) since this will be the truth, anyone who has a different view is dishonest; (7) "like it is" instead of "as it is" means that I, the speaker, am a plain, honest, blunt man of the people, and not one of those prissy-sissy types who go for "good form" and therefore don't like truth, and who therefore belong to an establishment which is also committed against the truth, etc. It isn't often that one can get so much self-praise, so much disparagement of others, and even a touch of malice into so few words that seem so strong and stark and Lincolnesque.

Let us be easy on ourselves at first by using more distant examples. I have long been struck by a couple of verbal habits of journalists re-
84

porting on Washington, D.C. When they speak of the acquaintances of high political figures, such as presidents, they rarely say "friends"; instead they use the strong term "close friends." Nearly every president is credited by the press with enough close friends to work him twenty-four hours a day keeping up with the closeness, or being smothered by it. Likewise, when any public figure is to be credited with any attitude other than indifference or agnosticism, the press always refers to him, not as "religious" but as "deeply religious." The upper echelons of government seem overrun with people engrossed in meditative and devotional exercises. Do these excessive phrases mean that journalists have lost all sense of the friendly and the religious and can convey the plain meaning only by exaggeration? Or do they crassly gratify a public who want not only a good thing but an extra large helping of a good thing? In either case, terms that should be used sparingly to conserve their power have been vulgarized; the squandering of significant words on quick kicks is a sad moral prodigality.

A concealed moral get-rich-quick scheme appears in our use of *challenge*—that term descended from a chivalry which we do not even admire. What do we say when we have got promoted, have got more pay, more territory, more subordinates, more power, and more glory? Not that what has come to us is an enlargement of the self and a boon to the ego. No, what has come to us is a *challenge*. By this word we become the humble knight with a sense of duty, obligated to respond with courage to the trial which is forced upon us. We are not a king coming into his kingdom, but a slender David selflessly facing Goliath.

Challenge is a standby of our society. It is likewise a standby of academe. Academe has a good deal of verbal traffic whose moral freight may not entirely correspond to the bill of lading. Aside from describing our mission as "training people to think"—a job description at which I raised an eyebrow in the preceding essay—consider our use of *memorization* as a bad word and *originality* as a good word. If we attack memorization as the learning process of dullards and drudges, a substitute for true thinking and speculation, we seem to ally ourselves with free, gay, dancing, leaping minds that soar lightly into high thought without grubby inhibitions. If we keep talking as if originality were a prime and unqualified virtue, we naturally ally ourselves with the fresh, spontaneous, and creative, and decry the dull and secondhand. But this two-pronged symbolic identification with genius may leave out most of the facts of life in the world of intelligent nongenius with which, even in higher education, we spend close to 100 percent of our time. To damn memorization is to ignore the fact that intelligence (not to mention wisdom) depends largely on what we

85

know, and that what we know is what we remember, whether our memory is lightning quick or goes by the steady labor called memorization. To scorn all memorization is not only to encourage ignorance; it stimulates that form of intellectual bumptiousness in which a person who does not remember very much is convinced that, because he has risen above memorizing, whatever comes into his head at random is unusually impressive as opinion and thought. Likewise with originality, of which we hear much in colleges and universities; we tend to confer an exclusive value upon what is truly possessed by an infinitesimally small number of people. This either depresses the majority needlessly, or, what is worse, inspires a quest of originality in persons unequipped for it. Hence much of pretentiousness. Hence a student's taking of every untutored notion, every uncriticized flurry of the ego, as a symptom of originality which deserves a public hearing—with some anguish to fellow students and instructors.

Another frequent figure in academic verbal traffic is *leadership*. We talk about the need of training for leadership, and I don't think I have ever heard anyone question the need. Yet I have long had a feeling that there is something here which won't quite hold up under inspection. I have toyed with the idea of pushing a paradox and proclaiming that what we really need to train people for is followership. I would rush to explain, if I could before a riot broke out, that by followership I meant acquiescence in corporate decisions that have been reasonably made, and identifying and giving up oppositionism that comes from love of display, of profit, of wilfulness, or from some other gratification of one's own ego. But if I praise followership, I become just a dictator looking for subservience, so I will forgo the pleasures of the shock method. I trace one doubt about leadership-training to the fact that in a real sense a leader, like a poet, is born and not made; that is to say, leadership lies in certain facets of personality which precede training and are not much altered by training. Another doubt comes from the fact that leadership is morally neutral; we can have good leadership in good, or good leadership in evil. Presumably we would not wish to train a leadership which would make evil more effective in the world. If then we come around and say that we only want to train leadership for the good, I cannot see that that means anything more than providing the prospective leaders, if we have identified them, with the customary educational experience of knowledge, general and concentrated, which we somehow hope will sharpen, in all our students, an ability to recognize the good and a devotion to it.

The verbal traffic on campus is often tied in with the flow of words downtown. When we treat memorizing as if it were an evil, we are only making a specific application of a general idea that permeates our air: that drudgery is not for free men, and that work itself is neither very pleasant nor very necessary. This view is implicit in nearly all the advertising that has to do with personal life, for instance that which treats premature retirement as an escape rather than a danger. Several years ago a salesman for the psychedelic religion, as he called it—he appeared to think of himself as a sort of founding apostle of the faith— assured an audience that it is perfectly all right to spend time taking drug-powered "trips" because fortunately there isn't very much work to be done any more. Now when a man peddles this sort of thing to a thousand people paying to hear it, he naturally begins to take a dim view of work. The trouble is that when we use the word *work* we do not distinguish between labor of excessive intensity and duration, which we have mostly done away with, and a regular activity which for most human beings is utterly essential, either as an escape from ourselves, or more important as a molding of the selves into a form that we do not have to escape from. A loss of hard work is a main source of a hard life.

Compare our use of the word *progress*, which for many people means a self-congratulatory conviction that we have improved greatly upon the past, and upon the Victorian age in particular. This crush of verbal traffic is always passing a somewhat smaller flow in the opposite direction: here we find the "good old days" crowd who believe that history is running downhill and that we have the unhappiness to exist in a very deplorable present. On the one hand we look down on the past; on the other we look down on the present. In either case we get an easy lift by going where the traffic is going; it's much more fun than to stop dead, face both past and present, and recognize, perhaps with pain, the contradictions within both, and the strange mixture of losing and gaining, or simply the neutral change, by which one age merges into another.

Then, in today's verbal traffic, take that old bus crowded with free-loaders, "the evils of society." This has become such a standard way of being on a good side that one finds it even in freshman themes. The user becomes the virtuous scourge of society, the independent man spotting fraud. Well, there are evils in society, obviously; but it is much too easy to talk about these out of context, to imply that they are quickly removable, and indeed sometimes that society itself is a removable evil. The fact is that as long as there are more than two people in the world, society irremovably exists and its influence is indispensable. One would like the noble fellow crying out about the evils of society to acknowledge the total problem—the very difficult one of maintaining essential social order without its becoming oppressive. But if the critic did that, he would give up his exhilarating one-way ride as a freewheeling crusader. The same person is likely, in his verbal traffic, to get a good deal of mileage out of *police brutality*. Such a critic rarely acknowledges that, given the imperfections of human nature, an enforcement agency seems necessary, and that the problem is the terribly difficult one of getting human enforcement without inhumane force. It is easy to attack brutality, which no one can be for; one can be on the right side, expect approval, and even indulge one's own punitive impulse all at the same time. The price of these advantages is leaving the painfully difficult problem untouched.

Let us turn to a much less localized and less contemporary form of aroused virtue harassing vice. I have in mind that familiar figure in the verbal traffic of condemnation—*hypocrisy*. For a long time it never occurred to me to inspect the freight being carried by this traffic. I simply assumed that Molière's *Tartuffe* told the whole story of hypocrisy. Then I had a strange experience. I ran into several instances in which hypocrisy was attacked by a person of bad manners, indeed, a boorish person. You see what happened: rude people identified hypocrisy with good manners they did not possess. Were they right? A boor is not necessarily a fool, alas. Can manners be construed as hypocrisy, and if so, should they be eliminated? Take so conventional a courtesy as "good morning." Would it be better—would I be a better person, and therefore would things in general be better—if, instead of saying "good morning," I said, "Bad luck to you" or "I hope you break a leg today" or "I can't stand the sight of you"? It hardly seems that such a greeting would make the world a better place. If, then, manners contain something of hypocrisy, are we saying "Up hypocrisy"?

There is, of course, a way around this dilemma. Good manners are morally a symbolic acknowledgment of our willingness to please others, to make concessions to them, to grant that they have certain rights and privileges—in a word, to practice a gracious yielding which may make life less tense and harsh. They are a form of humility, a discipline of the self, a subduing of its impulse to come first, to push, to be on top. Our man with no manners may insist that these impulses— the raw feelings of attack and conquest—are the only reality, and that keeping them in check is only pretense and affectation. Maybe, then, putting oneself in a secondary position, withholding assertiveness and animosity, is hypocrisy. But here we can distinguish between two hypocrisies. One kind practices an injurious deception: it seeks to profit the self by bamboozling others. The second kind practices an innocent deception: it seeks to gratify others by restraining the self. Hence just being against hypocrisy is too easy, and it may be self-indulgent,

88

because it leaves out real ramifications of meaning. Our bad-mannered people who are so harshly down on hypocrisy are really justifying their own raw impulse to ride roughshod over the rest of the world. On the other hand they are also implicitly laying claim to a positive virtue—namely, forthrightness, candor, honesty. They proclaim themselves, in a word, men of integrity.

Integrity is of course a "good word"; it denotes a virtue that we can hardly be against; and there may seem little ground for subjecting it to our inspection of verbal traffic. But let me quote a remark made to me by a colleague commenting on another colleague of ours: "He is a man of integrity. I wonder why he is so hard to take." The answer here was not hard to find: for our colleague, integrity meant not only acting unambiguously in accord with his belief, without tempering it to any prevailing winds of fashion, but treating his own belief as an absolute that had equal claims on everybody else. His belief made ours inadequate or untrustworthy. His integrity called our integrities in question, made them seem dubious. I began to wonder whether, in the very nature of what we call integrity, there is something which, if not formally guarded against, engenders self-assurance and rigidity. Integrity means completeness or wholeness; it means having the quality of an integer; an integer is a whole number; and it makes us think instinctively of oneness or singleness. In integrity one does not profess one belief and act on another; belief and action are identical, are one. It suddenly occurred to me that this comes rather close to what we call the "single-track mind." We can see, I think, how a certain kind of personality could easily jump over from moral wholeness or oneness to single-track mindedness, from an excellence to a petrified version of excellence, or plain rigidity. Here I am simply noting the ironically short step from being incorruptible to being inflexible and thus unpalatable, or even, on occasion, unbearable.

Again, integrity may become a kind of banner that we wave; we announce publicly and loudly that the quiet little voice within makes us leap into combat. It tends to be a conspicuous leap, with reporters and cameramen around. Integrity becomes not a quality that we earn by long moral growing pains, and privately hope that we may have at least part of the time, but a sort of decoration or a colorful insignia or a flashing toplight, like that on a police patrol car, by which we acquire special distinction and privilege. Here comes a man of integrity, everyone look out. If he is abusing institutions, officials, or people of different convictions, he has an especial right not to be considered wrong. If in this way integrity may become an article for display, in another way it may become a defensive strategy. If things are not going very well, if our defects catch up with us, if some nemesis threatens, we may feel the clarion call of integrity—to take up for some difficult cause, to defend what looks indefensible, to promote a belief or practice that outrages the immediate world. Then the axe that falls falls on the neck of a man who has given his all for a cause, not of one who did not give his all for the job or whose all was too small. Exit has been ennobled. Samuel Johnson, thinking of a politician he did not admire, once wittily asserted, "Patriotism is the last refuge of a scoundrel." Likewise integrity can become the last refuge of a mediocrity.

What I have called defensive integrity can clearly become aggressive. Our age seems to supply mechanisms or adopt attitudes which give certain advantages to the aggressor as against the object of aggression. All teachers and students know about the college class which is made miserable by the single member who on every issue insists on expressing himself vehemently and often quarrelsomely; nine times out of ten this difficult person, whether he knows it or not, is simply carrying out acts of aggression against the immediate community. What gives him a certain opening and protection is the concept of freedom of speech. My point, I need hardly add, is not that freedom of speech is bad, but that, like integrity, it can be used as a front, perhaps unknowingly, by individuals less interested in the truth of which freedom is the handmaiden, than in triumph or polemics or even in giving pain or inflicting injury. Dirty-word campaigns, which we all know, invoke freedom while reflecting little more than a desire to inflict pain on others; sometimes, when dirty-word operations purport to be literary, they betray that shortage of talent which often expresses itself in resentful aggressiveness. While our devotion to freedom is beneficial to the aggressor—be he entrepreneurial, wilful, resentful, or malicious —we have considerable difficulty if we seek freedom from him. If a person demands freedom to smoke in a full room, we tend to regard it as a legitimate right; if a person seeks freedom from another's smoke, he is likely to seem a finicky oddball. I need hardly mention the enormous difficulties we run into if we try to have freedom from billboards, freedom from telephone solicitation, freedom from noise. Antipollutionists on the auditory front seem only to shoot at distant rarefied targets like the sst, and to be deaf to the maddening circumambient snarl of firecracker car motors, motorcycles, and outboard motors.

Enough. I have wanted only to suggest how our application of such indispensable value-words as integrity and freedom can become infused with self-protection, self-deception, and self-aggrandizement. Human aggressiveness is ingenious in adopting the protective coloring

90

of respected concepts, that is, in running with the day's verbal traffic.

We have been looking, however, not at vice but at a kind of slipup, frequently unrecognized by us who slip, and hoping only to shed a little light. With light, presumably, a man would not willingly use the term "close friendship" to describe anything from random congeniality to experienced intimacy, or fall into any easy contempt for all pasts or for whatever present he happens to be living in, or let his casual usage imply that leisure is an unqualified blessing, and work or even drudgery an unmitigated evil. He would not really want to make himself feel good inside by speaking of everyone not positively an atheist as "deeply religious," or by presenting a proud and joyful acceptance of power and prestige as a humble acceptance of a "challenge." If he is a teacher, he will not publicly present the inevitably restricted and often inescapably pedestrian task of spreading knowledge in his own field as a bringing forth of originality, a training of people to think, and a production of leaders.

What I am driving at is the way in which the employment of certain popular words and phrases lets us play tricks on ourselves—the trick of ignoring the total situation or our own actual motives, and hence the trick of thinking well of ourselves and, above all, feeling good about ourselves. The use of the right term puts us easily on the right side. We can join a chorus against memorization, police methods, the evils of society, the tools of war, and revengefulness, and perhaps without knowing it grow in our own esteem, or invite the esteem of others. By latching on to key status terms we practice, to paraphrase Thorstein Veblen, the conspicuous assumption of merit, or, in a homelier economic figure, we flash our psychological or moral credit cards. It is hard to be for hypocrisy—though I have taken the calculated risk of sketching how it might be done—yet in abusing hypocrisy there may be a kind of unearned moral increment or a tax-exempt profit. All such seizures of rectitude are versions of what in the Sermon on the Mount was called praying "in the corners of the streets," where we "may be seen of men." So by announcing our integrity we may be seeking a moral protective coloration for our inflexibility or our wilfulness or our sheer stubbornness. The man of integrity may become the public or the professional man of integrity, self-conscious in his role, rather self-congratulatory about it, and obliquely inviting admiration. Must we not always take a second look at the man who calls a press conference to announce that his conscience (or his principles) compels him to act in such and such a way? Once he is conscious of conscience, may he not be putting the dress of virtue upon some purely habitual or obsessive course of action, or upon some other compulsion that is rather less noble? Does not the

91

true man of conscience remain silent about his motives and leave them to the estimate of others? Integrity, finally, may be the presentable public face of sheer combativeness, of the spirit of animosity and injuriousness that we call aggressiveness, of liking to push people around. Here we enter that always sad, and sometimes terrifying, realm in which antagonism and a desire to hurt take on the name of freedom, and the garment of liberty barely covers a naked impulse to feel power by wounding.

At times, then, the moral freight in fashionable verbal traffic—the real complications in the thing spoken of, and the hidden profit for the speaker—is different from what we suppose or expect. Happily it is not always thus. There are people who carry on both daily chores and special tasks but do not inflate them with ennobling terms. There are people who can perceive ills without bursting into the language of instant remedies, or into the severe polemics that spring from a total faith in one's own rectitude. There are critics whose words neither parade their own righteousness nor assume the lack of it in others. There are men of strong convictions whose words are generous to other men, who reflect on their own shortcomings more than they denounce the vices of others. There are believers in liberty who practice deference to others, and who in deed and word master the highest liberty which distinguishes the human from the bestial—the liberty to restrain aggressive impulses. There are men of integrity who do not announce their integrity, who act and speak quietly and unostentatiously. There are men of integrity who are witty and gracious, urbane and charitable. They provide the models for the civilized style that we need if we are to live with one another.

9
Clichés and
Anticlichés
Critics and Others

The critic is unlike the poet and the literary historian in that, in the esteem of the world in which he is known, his position jumps up and down like a nervous needle on an auto mechanic's ignition-testing apparatus. The poet, true, had his hard days, from Plato to the Puritans, but now, surely, he is completely out of the moral doghouse and the financial garret. If he does not always live like a resident artist in a Renaissance palazzo or in a well-heeled university, still he has a lifetime commuter's ticket to the White House (whether or not he quickly jumps aboard when the train is called). The historian has survived the abuse of Lemuel Gulliver, the sneer of a sort of modern horseless-carriage Gulliver who said that "History is bunk," and the contumely of a school of critics who have called him a mere antiquarian. In a world increasingly attracted to a relativistic understanding of truth, he is strongly entrenched as the explicator of many varieties of transitory experience. (But this is only an anticipatory note. The next essay looks at the problem of historians in our day, the essay after that theorizes about the temperamental differences between historians and critics.)

The critic survives too, but in a market where he may be bought or dumped with equal celerity as passions fluctuate. On the one hand Oscar Wilde has lauded the critic as an artist in his own right, and if this seems only another Wildian effort to startle and provoke, it is interesting that in 1939 André Gide, speaking to Claude Mauriac, "sang the praises of critics," terming them the "equals of artists," and calling an essay of Sainte-Beuve's "as fine as the greatest poem." Precisely, the literary historian is likely to reply severely: the critics mold an image of themselves out of the very work they are supposed to be criticizing selflessly. But if from one side the critic is damned as being

93

too creative, from the other side he is even more strongly damned as a made-over creator who failed to create. Disraeli asks, "You know who the critics are?" and replies, "The men who have failed in literature and art." Shelley is fiercer: "As a bankrupt thief turns thief-taker in despair, so an unsuccessful author turns critic." Naturally, then, Byron urges, "Believe a woman or an epitaph . . . before, / You trust in critics." It gets still better in the twentieth century, for which Roy Campbell speaks most warmly and richly. Campbell cries out against "the irrelevant and parasitical literature of theory, explanation, and criticism which entirely overshadows and dwarfs the creative work"; "the meaningless technical jargon of contemporary criticism"; "the uncreative majority of politico-critical pedants who really for the time being call the tune"; "crossword-conscious professors demanding . . . to be *puzzled* by poetry which is more difficult to read than write." And so on, and on.

Yet the critic lives on, whether he is detestable or lovable, whether he is uncritically creative while purporting to be a dispassionate analyst, or has fled to criticism as the refuge of the uncreative man. The critic continues to exist because all of us who read are critics. We are critics whenever we try to interpret or explain or judge, or to find a rational form for our likes and dislikes, our approvals and disapprovals —in a word, whenever we go beyond the pure, spontaneous feeling by which we respond directly to the work read. The critic is simply a specialist, not in the sense that he is different from, or does something different from, other readers, but in that he exercises more regularly than they a certain human impulse and aspires to do it in an orderly and principled way. A specialist exists only because Everyman cannot do equally well everything that Everyman can do. But he would cease to exist if Everyman did not want to do, or to have done, what the critic does. At present, however, the human impulse to inspect the mechanics and the quality of imaginative action is quite lively. So the critic continues among us, and he appears to have tenure in our society.

As a specialist with tenure, he has certain responsibilities. At this point one might put together, as from a cloud of smoke on Mt. Sinai, a pretty solemn decalogue of specific responsibilities—to protect excellence, train taste, guard culture, save the humanities, detect the timeless amid the flux of history, and so on. But I want to avoid grandeur, which easily blows up into the highfalutin, and to name only one responsibility—one that is not very resounding nor spectacular nor breathtaking, that could not get headlines, and that may not seem even to have the high tone called for by so serious a word as *responsible*. I

94

mean, simply, the responsibility to avoid filtering criticism through intellectual clichés. His responsibility is analogous to that of the general public addressed in the two preceding essays, but because he is special rather than general, his is greater. The critic ought to be responsible not only for avoiding fashionable clichés but, more than that, for resisting them. He ought to try to avoid a patter of his own, and he ought to oppose all the kinds of patter that seem to put the master patterer, and all who patter after him, in intellectual control of a wholly intelligible world.

The natural prey of the critic should be all the handy verbal tools that have become too much of a vogue to remain critical. C. P. Snow, however suspect he may be because he has become a vogue himself, is surely right when he says: "Of course, as soon as a critical slogan is put forward, it is the easiest thing in the world for it to spread. We are all much more suggestible than we like to think. Fashions in criticism are accordingly too easy to start, and dangerous when they are on the move. With the catchword *bitter* in the back of one's mind, one can read a book and find the bitterness in every line—and spare oneself the trouble of looking for anything else." Exactly. When a reader reads in an atmosphere created by clichés, he will have to be all but a genius to fight his way through to an independent view of the book, not to mention finding in it a reality which is simply not identified by any of the clichés in the air around him.

Take a slogan word that is almost the opposite of *bitter*, that is, *compassionate*. I feel as though I had read a thousand reviews of novels in which *compassionate* was used as the term of highest praise for the novelist. Here the cliché reflects a confusion between literary and social values, and indeed deepens it. It is not the artist's business to be compassionate any more than it is his business to be uncompassionate or callous or bitter; it is his business to encompass as much of his chosen reality as he can, not to defend it nor damn it nor feel sorry for it. It is his business to have and express a vision, not to stroke brows nor hold hands. If we keep praising him for compassion, we are unconsciously trying to pressure the artist into being a visiting nurse. And, worse than that, the cliché helps create a climate in which it will be increasingly difficult to read Aeschylus, Racine, Shakespeare, and indeed nearly every other great writer—the end result of reducing the encompassing to the compassionate.

Take another kind of slogan word, *absurd*, which is used with overwhelming uncritical frequency. One can turn to essay after essay and find writers asserting, as if it were an unarguable truth, that experience is absurd, life is absurd, destiny is absurd, and we are absurd; and then proceeding to explain how not only a parade of new books, but a

95

great many from earlier centuries, demonstrates this absurdity. In expressing my dismay at this rush to be absurd, I do not hope to dispose of the absurditarian position or positions (though often they seem to rephrase only a common irony of life). The problem is rather the quasi-critical taking over of a fashionable word, the begging of the philosophical issue, being in the swim, and seeming to have an up-to-date key for virtually all literary locks. In *The Wild Duck* Ibsen took the word *ideal,* which had become a cliché for Gregers Werle and even for Ibsen himself, and exposed it; we can see this clearly, because *ideal* is not now fashionable. What we need is a picture of a modern Gregers Werle enforcing "the absurd" on everyone around him and thus messing up their world. It might reduce the number of people running around and uncritically seeming to take pleasure in finding absurdity everywhere, and thus helping spread a rigid unilateral view of reality. Consider the slogan word *life,* which usually gets into literary quasi criticism in the form of assertions that so-and-so "is on the side of life," which is good, and so-and-so is not, which is not good. Some people reduce literary criticism to little more than running through literary works and quickly dividing authors and characters into the quick and the dead, or the life-lovers and the death-seekers. These clichés create an intellectual melodrama no more sophisticated than any popular melodrama of good guys and bad guys. For *life,* like other clichés, makes simple classifications but prevents essential distinctions. There are lives and lives, and deaths and deaths; one may live badly or die well; one may kill from malice or lust, or to survive; one may crave death from inadequacy or disorder or from concern for others; one may crave life but accept death because one hears an imperative. The critic ought to press constantly for such discriminations, for discrimination is the true alternative to the cliché.

The clichés about life, including the pseudoreligious "reverence for life," are in part a development of popular Freudianism. One need not be anti-Freudian, nor unappreciative of the greatness of Freud, to feel dismay at the facile Freudian clichés that overflow in both published criticism and classroom criticism. The clichés betray not only the fondness for simplifying thought about human reality by serving it up in a few handy categories, but a very old habit of mind which we may have thought we had outgrown—a weakness for allegorical interpretation. Everybody knows the half-dozen basic terms by which a multitude of motives, of complex responses, of aspirations, of beliefs, all the sources of human richness, are reduced to automatic, single-valued reactions that seem to do away with uncertainty, ambiguity, and mystery and render the master of clichés the easy, pigeonholing master of human reality. Even more than medieval allegory, our popular Freudian clichés not only reduce innumerable phenomena to several very limited psychic meanings, but cut back hundreds of diverse objects and figures to one or two simple physiological significations. In the interest of avoiding a deceptive simplicity we ought, in the words of Saul Bellow's Herzog, to "resist this creeping psychoanalysis of ordinary conduct."

Yet we are so given to clichés that we can make them out of the very contradictoriness of life. Reading Nikos Kazantzakis's spiritual journal *Report to Greco,* I came across this sentence: "I felt that love, death, and God were one and the same." Within twenty-four hours, reading a modern essay on comedy, I found the author commending a couple of characters in fiction because "they both know that the body, love, and death are all three the same thing." When I was assured one day of the identity of love, death, and God, and the next day of the identity of love, death, and the body, I suddenly realized that for a long time I had been coming upon passages making such identifications; my two finds simply confirmed an uneasiness with something that had long seemed too easy. (How much the making of paradoxical equations is in the air is revealed when it hits not only the essayist who tends to echo the sounds around him, but also a very original man like Kazantzakis.) Now whether we equate love and death and the body or love and death and God—putting the two trinities together makes God the same as the body, which to many observers will seem another cliché—we are, of course, utilizing a valuable mode of thought: the discovery of subterranean links or even bonds between matters traditionally taken to be separate or unrelated or even antithetical. Out of this process come paradoxes that embody new insights. But then the intellectual labor or the imaginative leap creating the paradox is left behind, and the mere words of it become over-the-counter gimmicks for surprising the uninitiate without bringing him to mental life, where distinctions must be made. A really deadening cliché is one that started as a live paradox.

Noncritical or anticritical clichés may have to do not only with the content or the tone of literature but also with the teaching, the nature, and the role of literature. Around English departments we often hear the cliché that a teacher should be turned loose on classes to teach only what pleases or interests him, or, even worse, what he's doing research on. It is possible that with such a franchise an instructor may bring an inspiriting zest into the educational arena. But the price of his freedom may well be the enslaving of his classes to special tastes and interests. The instructor knows no shackles, but he puts his own brand marks on his flocks; they bleat and moo only in echo of the master's voice. The demanding alternative to the autonomy of the instructor's preferences, passions, and research projects is the unyielding sense that, quite outside his own heart with its fervent beat, lies an objective body of literature—a period, a type, or a canon—that needs to be considered with as much completeness and detachment as possible if one is to train, not special pleaders, but cultivated human beings. Here again we can recall Gide's aphorism that culture begins only when we approach what we do not already like. That should be a good brake on pedagogical wilfulness, which is one form of uncriticalness.

If one cliché makes us free not to approach what we don't already like, another treats literature as a weapon against what we do already dislike. To many academic minds literature exists as a sort of truculent rebel bedeviling the professor's own favorite targets—particularly and most frequently the bourgeoisie and the world of convention. All the pseudocritical bandying about of banalities on the evils of convention and the virtues of anticonventionality is a substitute for the much harder critical task of distinguishing among conventions which are indispensable, those which are innocuous, and those which have served their day and may well be discarded. It ignores the fact of life that much more than half of all our conduct is conventional and has to be. In America it is a convention that we drive on the right-hand side of the road, and in England on the left; in either country the man whose integrity demands that he be unconventional may find that honesty is not really the best policy. In a university it is a convention to import visiting speakers. If one is trapped in the same room with them when they are lecturing, it is conventional not to eat lunch, order drinks, play poker, make love, change one's clothes, practice a musical instrument, or watch a horse race on television; and if one is despite oneself put to sleep, it is conventional to try to look awake. Now it may well be that the human spirit would be greatly enlarged if some of these conventions were done away with. My sole point is that the critic who has escaped from clichés must work at discriminating which ones deserve retention or rejection. Or he might, with Goncharov in the novel *Oblomov,* speak of a "desultory desire to conform to the inevitable proprieties, if only to be free of them." *There* is a paradox that is not a cliché and that is correspondingly perceptive: desultory conformity as the avenue to freedom. Conformity, however, is often a bad word that evokes cliché attitudes of dissent. Here an aphorism by Mitchell Morse is apposite: "compulsive disobedience is a form of intellectual dependence." Goncharov and Morse provide an antidote to the view, often circulated around academe, that conventions are a sinister tyranny by which someone is putting something over on us.

The cliché anticonventionality which often shows up in literary

98

studies may take the form of abuse of the bourgeoisie, as if it were an undifferentiated lumpish entity that all free spirits should unite to disparage if not abolish. Again the easy cliché frees us from the difficult obligation of distinguishing bourgeois from bourgeois in that incredibly large and complex social category. Viewed neutrally, the bourgeois is presumably the noncreative, materially oriented man. The critic needs to give direction in seeing where the bourgeois comes in on the immense spectrum of possibilities in his class. Is he the noncreative man who hates creation, burns books, censors the unfamiliar (or the too familiar)? He sometimes is. Is he the callous or hostile philistine who thinks artists are troublemakers and finds security in clichés? He sometimes is. Or is he the noncreative man who is the enlightened consumer for the creative man, the patron, the receptive audience, the public which combines its historic stability with exceptional accessibility and without which the artist might be largely talking to himself? He sometimes is this, too. The critic is obligated to challenge any clichés which free their user from making such distinctions.

Though the critic is bound to practice dissent against the favorite clichés of his time, it is by now apparent that dissent itself may become a cliché. (Standardized abuse of the conventional and the bourgeois are subdivisions of the dissent cliché.) I am not talking about social or political dissent, which is not my problem, but about the academic cliché which makes it the nature of literature—and hence of writers and students of it—to be always against something. This cliché has a good run in colleges and universities because it hits students just when, as an inevitable part of the growing-up process, they are ready to be against things in general, and literary sponsorship can make even the most mechanical anti-Establishmentarianism seem like a noble crusade. Lest I seem to be dissenting against dissent instead of against a cliché, let me hasten to add that if "assent" were a popular cliché in literary study, I would have a paragraph about it. But if my radar in the atmosphere of literary ideas is reliable, *assent* is a word hardly heard, and *dissent* is everywhere a bargain item.

If one proposes that it is the business or nature of literature to engage in dissent (or, for that matter, assent), one is trying to make it over into journalism, propaganda, topical pleading. If he succeeded in persuading a writer that this was his mission, he would make it ever so much harder for the writer to get out of his own decade and into the company of the great. For it is the business of the writer, and the essence of literature, not to dissent or assent, but, as I said earlier, to discover and frame artistically a vision of reality. It is the dissent cliché that makes one kind of professorial critic of Joyce's *Portrait of the Artist* praise Stephen only for his negations—for being antichurch, anti-Ireland, antifamily—and forget that this is only one-half, the preliminary half, of the picture. This kind of critic is enchanted with Stephen's saying *non serviam*—I will not serve—and thus becoming a modern Lucifer; the dissent cliché seems to make us quite sentimental about the devil. But our dissent man never notices, or honestly forgets, two important passages in the chapter in which Stephen finds and accepts his vocation as artist. One passage mentions "the end he had *been born to serve* yet did not see"; in the other, Stephen sees the image of Daedalus winging upward over the waves and asks if this is not "a prophecy of the end he had *been born to serve* and had been following through the mists of childhood and boyhood." "The end he had *been born to serve*": the inevitability of serving exactly balances the *non serviam*. The cliché of the artist as rebel embraces, at most, half the truth.

The cliché view that literature and the writer are naturally allied with dissent opens up the strange fact that liberty itself can become a cliché. Now this is a delicate subject, and to avoid misunderstanding one had better declare explicitly that freedom—of thought and choice —is a human necessity. But freedom becomes a cliché when it means freedom *from* thought, when the simple calling for freedom usurps all the energy that should go also into examining freedom, defining its ends, and criticizing its uses. Crying aloud for freedom requires no talent; anyone can do it. The critic must go further. In literature the most characteristic invocation of freedom takes the form of fighting censorship. This has to be done. But criticism starts where censorship leaves off. Today censorship, simply by disappearing, has left the critic with more than usually demanding tasks. Take all those naughty deeds, naughty feelings, and, above all, naughty words that now leap friskily out in public nakedness after several centuries of a less assertive existence beneath the tempering drapery of implication and indirection. They confront the critic with an enormous problem—rather like having to decide, at a nudist camp, which persons, if they were dressed, would look grimy, which ones stodgy, which ones elegant. For naughty words can be used with equal ease and surprisingness by great artists, by pretenders, by vindictive people, by humorless people, by sick people, by trivial people, and by nitwits. The critic who has got beyond the clichés of freedom must now judge its results—must discriminate, with anguish of mind and soul, between uncensored art and uncensored junk. It is a touchy business, and it sometimes appears to attract less energy than it should. Occasionally I have the impression that habitual dissenters are happier if they can still dig up some traces of censorship to fight. It is easier to cry out against repression than to judge the no longer repressed.

Besides, the criticism itself is likely to seem repressive, an act of infidelity to our own times. A very interesting kind of cliché is the self-congratulatory one by which not only our own time, but every time, triumphs over the time before. Sometimes this is the eternal one-up-manship among centuries; sometimes it is the touching self-esteem by which each period places itself at a new aesthetic and cultural apex. In either case a historical cliché gives an easy victory over an adversary that has difficulty in talking back. The eighteenth century scorned the seventeenth for its passion and disorder, which seemed to have been cured by the rules of the couplet. The romantic period damned the neoclassical period for rigidity, frigidity, and inhumanity, which seemed to be symbolized in the rules of the couplet. And everyone knows what we damn the nineteenth century for—for all the imperfections and errors and perversities which we call Victorianism. That sad world, we are fairly sure, was not honest and wild and free, like us. Another cliché of historical gamesmanship is to render our approval of some past work by showing that it really conforms to some cliché of our own—that is, by being absurd, bitter, compassionate, life-worshipping, and so on. Notice what we have done to Shakespeare's shrew since the category of shrews has become unfashionable. Now we do not attribute Katherine's troubles to a faulty personality but blame them on someone else—a tyrannical father and a bitchy little sister; Katherine, starved for love, is only a modern problem child. From these clichés we leap to still another: the feministic triumphs in the war of the sexes make us habitually impute weakness to men and power and guile to women. So what happens to *The Taming?* Now it is Katherine who is taming Petruchio; she only pretends to agree with him in order to gain power over him, and her substantial closing speech on the duty of wives is only a prolonged ironic smirk at the deluded male.

The criticism that undercuts clichés and offers the sudden thrill of an insight beyond fashion keeps cropping up, often in unexpected places. In an interview in *Partisan Review* Rolf Hochhuth, author of *The Deputy*, says: "I consider it fatal if we allow ourselves to be influenced by the chitchat of the editorial writers about our living in an age of the masses, which, naturally, is true to some extent. But we must not allow this to induce a person to think only of his impotence, and not of the fact that as an individual he must always bear the responsibility not only for his family but for the entire community." A helpful recoil against clichés about the masses, and about the powerlessness of the individual in a mass age. In a novel, of all places, we find a similar recoil against the cliché view of relativism as essentially a valuelessness that forbids discrimination and judgment. The narrator in John Barth's

The Floating Opera has a high moment of discovery: "if there are no absolutes, then a value is no less authentic, no less genuine, no less compelling, no less 'real,' for its being relative! It is one thing to say 'values are only relative'; quite another, and more thrilling, to remove the pejorative adverb and assert, 'there *are* relative values!' " Again, the narrator in Saul Bellow's *Herzog*: "We must get it out of our heads that this is a doomed time, that we are waiting for the end, and the rest of it, mere junk from the fashionable magazines. . . . People frightening one another—a poor sort of moral exercise." This is a tonic challenge of the familiar clichés of self-pity. *Herzog* offers us still another: "The day is fast approaching . . . when only proof that you are despairing will entitle you to the vote, instead of the means test, the poll tax, the literacy exam. You must be forlorn." For such freshness of thought, one must be grateful. Note that in all these passages it is creative writers who are functioning as critics.

Some clichés alluded to here, though they have secondary echoes in literature, deal primarily with attitudes to experience and the state of the world. But literature is so entwined with life that willy-nilly the literary critic is often a critic of life. Indeed his eternal vigilance against the cliché is, in effect, a vigilance against the deformations of life that the pounding of a cliché can bring about. Take all the clichés about the failure of communication in modern life: if they are dinned into people often enough, without antidote, this can so mold their sensibilities as to make them incapable of communication. By the repetitive motions of language they can be hypnotized into accepting the barrier of self as final, and thus into failing in the obligation to try to breach it. Again, there is peril in the cliché use of the word *tragedy*, by which I mean our tireless, indiscriminate application of the word to all kinds of distresses and misfortunes, to outer slipups and inner flaws. The peril is that in lumping all such events together as tragedy we finally lose the power to separate crass accident, malicious action, and the subtle self-deceptions and powerful promptings by which we create our own evil. And so we may become less and less able to recognize our own responsibility for what goes wrong and for doing wrong. Another cliché that often comes up in connection with undefined tragedy is the word *waste*. In fact, the deploring of waste, especially human waste, is a standardized public ritual for seeming high-minded without paying a high price for it. In the critic's view, the cliché may conceal an economic bias: we may be lamenting the loss of people before we have gained all we might from them. It may substitute tight accounting for accurate valuing, quantity of life for quality of being. It may blind us to the fact that prodigality may have its values as well as parsimony. It may help us forget that the theology of the full dinner pail, the center of possibly our highest faith now, may entail, as an inevitable consequence, the well-filled garbage can.

Here one or two qualifications are in order. One is that the cliché is rarely an untruth that is to be battered down; it is rather a half-truth that has become a best seller. Ironically it may even be a humble instrument of thought, or quasi thought, a superficial means of order without which thinking and its surrogates might be even more disorderly than they are. The problem is to keep it under surveillance, to prevent it from dominating all the realms of thought, and to make it yield to discrimination as often as is humanly possible.

For the true opponent of the cliché is discrimination, and not, as it might seem at a superficial glance, originality. Indeed the cliché is a mass-produced echo of some individual's real originality. We can avoid being parrots only by discrimination, which can be acquired. Strangely we spend little time praising discrimination, much time praising originality. This places needless strain on aspiring minds, which in pursuit of originality often struggle self-consciously into strained novelties. One can manage the semblance of originality without penetration or discrimination.

Yet originality is seductive, and its easiest answer to the cliché—far easier, and much more spectacular, than discrimination—is to come up sparkling with the anticliché. In this ploy you do not examine the cliché; you simply reverse it or turn it upside down or inside out. It is one of the methods of the literary *enfant terrible,* but the truth is that anyone can play at it. Everyman can thus be his own *enfant terrible.* If the cliché is that honesty is the best policy, the anticliché insists that policy makes the only honesty. It is not the letter that killeth, but the spirit that killeth. Sainthood comes, not from self-mortification, but from self-indulgence (especially of the more perverse sorts). Love is only a form of death (though it is the form that the uninstructed seem to prefer). Society must fear, not literature that has an excess of violence, but literature that is not violent enough. Cowardice is the only true bravery. Apply the rod, and spoil the child. Pope is the ultimate romantic poet. Don Juan is a selfless martyr to community health. Now this has come to be a pretty familiar way of getting around in the world. In literature the hero has been pushed into a decline, for we have invented the antihero. One wonders if the male is on the way out, for a critic has recently advanced the concept of the antimale. The novel has all but gone under, for we have invented the antinovel. I read recently a lengthy discussion of the art of antiart and another of the theater of antitheater. This will probably not stop until we have run through all the scales of possibility and created a new, tight, unyielding world of antitypes and antitruisms. (I have recently come across the following "anti-nouns," all used in literary pieces of the most unsmiling seriousness: "antipoetry," "antilyric," and "anti-Faust." Perhaps we are ready for an Anti-anti League.) These will be, not new truths, not new untruths, but a new flock of half-truths that are the other half of the old half-truths. They will sell. In other words, as some have already done, the anticlichés will themselves become clichés.

In trying to undercut the cliché—which is different from destroying it utterly or standing it on its head—the critic of course has to begin at home. He has much more humanity than is sometimes supposed, and it is in virtue of that humanity that he is likely to repeat himself, quote himself, drift into key terms, and then, in the final stage, count on the key terms to do the work as if, each time a key term is used, it made an incisive independent analysis of an issue. A few years ago the editor of a journal censured me for overuse of the word *mature*. I took thought and had to acknowledge, to myself at least, that perhaps that word had been coming out too easily; that though it does denote a virtue, I might, in calling on it, have begged the question instead of making a demonstration; and that I perhaps used it as a rod instead of as a probe. Again, I grew up, critically speaking, in a world in which irony was greatly valued as a literary characteristic, and I employed the term regularly. It took me a long time to realize that irony could be a too handy device for dispensing praise (and also for dispensing blame), and that the only hedge against a cliché usage was to regard irony as essentially a neutral device. As such it might be used, on the one hand, with great revelatory power, and might, on the other, be labored, contrived, an artifice more likely to astonish than to reveal. Again, I long thought of a sense of guilt as essential to the tragic hero and hence as not only identifying but beneficent. Hermann Hesse seemed to me wholly right in calling guilt the route to innocence. But then there were Hardy's Sue Bridehead and Duerrenmatt's Mr. Mississippi, in whom guilt led to sickness, and sickness to punitiveness, of oneself and even of others—to anything, indeed, but salvation. As often, the idea of guilt had become a cliché, the cliché was a half-truth, and I had to search for a more complex and demanding perspective.

I cite these instances in order to present as concretely as I can the process of identifying and revising clichés. One has to find examples close to home; in fact, the critic's only sure method of detecting and analyzing vice is introspection. Yet the truth is that seeing one's own clichés in perspective is a difficult assignment. We are all somewhat bound within our intellectual personalities, and our clichés mirror these personalities. If we recognize that our clichés naturally have a partisan role, we are better prepared to reduce their partisanship and to make them into uncommitted or unpredictable instruments that may surprise us instead of just gratifying our preconceptions. In this effort we exercise the practical self-criticism which is an important, and often neglected, duty of the critic. Though neither a tragic hero nor an intellectual Samson, he can occasionally enjoy some calm of mind, all fashion spent.

When the critic spots, and tries to control, his own trusty rods for measuring and whipping others, he is in a better moral position to expose the clichés of others. But even if he does remain partly blind to his own automatisms, he still needs to keep a sharp eye on the clichés around him—especially the ones that all the brighter people use as the latest currency of the mind. Literary clichés exert a powerful, if unrecognized, influence on our sense of reality—more so, I suspect, than political or economic or social clichés. For they help determine what we make of literature, and literature helps determine what we make of life. It does this, not by moralizing, not by being didactic, but by its extraordinary impact on the imagination. When this influence works through unexamined assumptions—the ones that tend to be in everybody's mouth, or in the best mouths—it can contribute to a grievously slanted sense of reality. The critic should keep trying to rebalance it. His efforts should reveal that he is not always the parasite, not always the artist manqué, not always a fanciful re-creator of others' creations, but is sometimes, in a small auxiliary way, responsible to the creative by trying to maintain its freedom from the modish which quickly becomes the shopworn.

IN THE STUDY:
HISTORICAL AND CRITICAL
APPROACHES

10
The Antiquarians
and the Up-to-Date
Attitudes toward History

One of the explicit themes in Robert Penn Warren's *All the King's Men* is the break, in our day, between men of action and men of thought. This split appears very sharply in our attitudes to history: there is a large congregation of the faithful to whom history is god, and an equally large, probably larger, brotherhood of skeptics to whom history is bunk. On the kneeling cushions before Clio are certain men of thought, or at least of a kind of thought; standing upright and saluting the last day on the engagement pad are the men of action, all muscles and nerves. From their opposite directions the historiophiles and the historiophobes threaten a balance of past and present that society needs—a harmony of the immediate and the experienced. When neither attitude to the past gets out of hand, that is, when historiolaters and historioclasts are each a goading minority rather than a controlling influence, a reciprocal process that may make us a little wiser is most likely to be operating as it should: the new modifies the remembered, and the remembered modifies the new.

Not all men of thought are historians, and not all historians are historiophiles. Yet it is the humanities which are always likely to get lopsided with antiquarianism, with a pale yet incurable monomania for setting a carefully delimited factual record straight; whereas the sciences and social sciences, feeding always upon new data, new points of view, and new methods, tend, despite the deprecation and regret of their wiser men, to give aid and comfort to a climate in which "it's the latest thing" betokens an authentic revelation from on high. With the speeding sciences the here-and-now men of action feel kinship; in this apparent piling of revolution on revolution they have the illusion of finding the theoretical justification for excluding as irrelevant everything that is not in and of the moment. Against this impetus to the unhistorical in the world of ideas, and to the antihistorical in the world of action, there have been reactions in the last few decades: such phenomena as "great books" courses for the world, and "humanities" courses for academe (not to mention a mild waterfall of foundation and even government funds intended to pump life into the humanities). Here we run into a nice problem: how can the professors of the humanities, who for a hundred years have been high-church antiquarians, that is, devoted to the past as past, ever persuade the up-to-date activists that history is meaningful, that is, that the past is present as well as past?

Several years ago, for instance, a "critic" (as opposed to a historian) said he wanted to "save the humanities," by which, I take it, he meant they should be more than a parade ground for the display of historiographic virtuosity, and hence able to defend themselves as having something to say to contemporary man. He referred primarily to literature, and he was simply asserting that it has values which transcend the elements of a work traceable to its background and its times (literary history) and to its author's life (biography). The repetition of this modest claim that art is art and must be meaningful as such and not as something else has led to occasional hullabaloo and to continual sniping, often in the form of misrepresentations peculiarly ironic.

The fashionableness of onslaughts against nonhistorical positions reveals the tenacity of the historiophile position in the humanities. The danger of the historiophile extreme is that it can sterilize important areas in higher education. Now, beside this professional antiquarianism there is a seriocomic lay antiquarianism (comic in appearance, serious in implication) which is perhaps what we get when its custodians lock up the past for solemn ritual play instead of making it meaningful. This lay antiquarianism makes a booming business of the manufacture of phony antiques—a paradoxical modishness of the outmoded which should really be understood as providing an innocuous way for up-to-the-minute-men to salute the past. It is a significant phenomenon, the susceptibility of the here-and-now race to a there-and-then façade, e.g., the olde gifte shoppe, that coy wench making like Clio and fixing to take the customer; the reassuring ties traced on chiseled headstones; the heirlooms displayed; the sites visited; the ideological genealogy which rigs up a respectable family tree for the hot conviction of the hour ("Washington said," "Mill said," etc.). The present is hardly in danger, of course; collecting Colonial argues no real convalescence from that provincialism in time which makes today's best seller a still better seller, and last year's best seller only a back number. Yet these

110

dabblings in the pseudohistoric and the quaint historic all evidence a real need—even in a society in which progress is virtually a religion.

Man needs the past, whether he knows it or not; he shies away from it partly because some specialists in it shy away from everything else. The problem of living in the present without ignoring the past is matched by the problem of having a historic sense without getting buried in history; the overall problem is to have a sense of the present and a sense of the past, and through both a sense of something more inclusive than either. What is contributed by a sense of the present hardly needs demonstration. But what are the products of the historic sense? These, perhaps: awareness of origins, perspective, humility. Each of these values is really a mean which must be placed against the distortion of it created by the two extreme attitudes to history of which we have spoken.

Take awareness of origin. Historiolatrous extreme: ancestor worship (the genealogy business); the genetic fallacy (sources and influences tell us all about a work of art). Historioclastic extreme: "Pappy is old-fashioned"; illusion of being self-made; illusion of the "new start." Mean: ability to distinguish essence from historical accident; knowledge of immanence of past in present. Or take perspective. Historiolatrous extreme: perspective is all; aesthetic and moral relativism; history of ideas as *summa*. Historioclastic extreme: every day a new woods to be lost in; each present an absolute. Mean: having perspective *on something,* on present man, who is seen, not merely with reference to his contemporariness, but with reference to his totality as sketched in history. Finally take humility. Historiolatrous extreme: "things aren't what they used to be"; retrospective arcadianism. Historioclastic extreme: present man as apex of evolutionary process; all pasts as "barbarous."

The mean? Can one define humility as a virtue for the nineteenth and twentieth centuries, in whose moral arithmetic humility equals Heep? (The tragic hero manqué, not venturing his pride and risking Nemesis, but disguising it in rags and forever fondling these grimy tatters in public.) Who can sink into despair but despise humility? (Having thus to invent naturalistic tragedy, in which downfall is inevitable but undeserved.) But humility as a mean is not creeping, or fawning, or standing pride on its head: rather it is a sense of incompleteness which mediates between complacency and wormishness. This sense of incompleteness is not sense of failure or loss of hope; it is not neurotic; it is historic. The historical orientation brings into focus other incompletenesses, and not only these, but also other strivings for completeness. It contributes to an image of complete man, an image which may never become actual but which must always define and direct the human effort at self-realization. Thus the historic sense, which means a full interplay of past and present, militates against both parochial vanity and the despair of truth or, in terms of time, against a shallow up-to-datism and a sterile antiquarianism.

11
Historian
and Critic
The Types

A few years ago the English critic John Holloway, in arguing a point, alleged that insofar as his arguments were "speculative," they were "dubious" and "precarious." Whatever the risks, the present essay is speculative. If this is a vice, there may be an advantage in it: in literary study as in life, one can hope that vice will have some perverse attraction for those who are exposed to it, and that it will turn out to be alluringly suggestive. Besides, when the subject is history and criticism, there may be another profit in the speculative: at least it will be a change from the more familiar mode, the querulous-polemic.

The basic premise is that the recent skirmishing, three or four decades of it, between literary history and literary criticism has psychological origins worth inspecting. In one sense this is perfectly obvious: the interplay between proponents of different positions begat considerable emotion, and the formal positions advanced were often compounded as much of feeling as of cool thought. For instance, an externalism that was felt to be absolute (historical method) stimulated, in reaction, an absolute internalism (the autotelic text: all ye need to know). But a theory of reaction is obviously introductory; it alludes to occasion rather than cause; and we must seek deeper grounds for the split in the ways of regarding literature. The speculative point is that these grounds are in the structure of the mind. This sounds portentous, and one can only hope that the following pages will make the phrase seem something more than a verbal flourish of trumpets.

The situation as felt thirty or forty years ago can be described in these words of Harry Levin: "The prevailing aim of literary historiography . . . was a kind of illustrated supplement to extraliterary history.

Academic research concentrated so heavily upon the backgrounds of literature that the foreground was all but obliterated." Now this passage refers, not to the 1920s and 1930s in America or England, but to events of more than half a century earlier in France. Levin goes on, "Flaubert's gloomy prediction, that literature would be absorbed by history, was all but realized," and records Flaubert's telling Turgenev that Sainte-Beuve and Taine shocked him because "they do not pay sufficient attention to Art, the work in itself." So the more recent reaction against the dominance of the historical approach echoes and enlarges an earlier one, just as contextualist, organicist, and formalist assumptions themselves develop from the work of earlier theorists— Coleridge, Hegel, Croce, Valéry. We can go still further back. Taine's doctrine of moment, race, and milieu extends, as we all know, the eighteenth-century method of justifying literary styles obviously not congruent with what were taken to be Greek and Roman canons. The Wartons, of course, were key figures in promoting the hypothesis of literature as characteristic of its age, and as manifesting the genius of that age. (One can see the shift in Shakespeare studies as the century went on.) Levin pushes the roots of the conception back to the quarrel of the ancients and moderns; its implicit conclusion "that each [work] was the unique creation of its period," he says, "had adumbrated a historical point of view." For this view Arnold Stein suggests a still subtler point of emergence: the theorizing about mental action which turned on the words "wit" and "judgment"—roughly the perception of resemblances and the detection of differences. In Donne's day, Stein says, various influences "gave judgment and the perception of differences a particular advantage," and "a certain sense of righteous self-confidence attached itself to the perception of differences." Here is a crucial idea, or at least a useful point of departure. To venture into hypothesis: the awareness of a power to apprehend differences, brought into formal, public existence by continual theorizing about it and about alternative ways of intuiting reality, would seem to be the precondition and the ground for the emergence of the historical point of view. Let us speak, in loose metaphor, of an instinct for differentiation: we may think of it as hibernating or lying dormant, as subordinate to other organizing principles, as having a static taxonomic function, and then, when circumstances focus it upon time, becoming hyperactive, absorbing vast amounts of intellectual energy, and coloring modes of thought or even rendering them dependent upon it. We have seen such a development in modern times: generally in the expansion of historical study since the Renaissance, but especially in the vast growth of literary history since the eighteenth century.

To continue with the psychological hypothesis, let us posit a counterimpulse or instinct, and call it the instinct for integration: that is, the tendency to see wholes, unities. Differentiation involves the pursuit of identity through an ever-increasing fragmentation, a detection of unlikeness between centuries, and parts of one century, and decades or even shorter periods; integration, the pursuit of identity through an eye focused on totalities, on unifying likenesses within apparent un-likenesses, on integers tending always to be more inclusive. In literary study, it appears to me, what we have for some decades called history and criticism represent generally, though not exclusively, these con-verse workings of the human mind; these opposing movements, one toward an atomization of authoritative time, the other toward the single vision *sub specie aeternitatis*.

The integrationist temper appears most obviously in the sense of the work itself as an integer, a oneness self-established rather than an assem-blage of elements that must be identified by trace-lines to their origins or counterparts elsewhere. Eliot praises Leone Vivante, the Italian phi-losopher, for asserting that in the poem "something comes into being which is new—in the sense that it cannot be explained by literary or other influences," including the biographical. (They both stress the underivability of Shakespeare.) The integrationist temper appears in the sense of a oneness of substance in works or forms traditionally seg-regated. Some years ago a gentleman of the *ancien régime* all but im-puted moral turpitude to a critic who had used the same criteria in writing about Hawthorne and Dostoevsky; the old gentleman could not understand the cast of mind which instinctively goes for the com-mon ground in works of different time and place. Cleanth Brooks undertook to demonstrate that the basic instruments of formalist criti-cism of poetry are equally applicable to poems of different ages with styles traditionally considered irreconcilable. Recently Leone Vivante has gone even further in the integrationist direction. After quoting from hundreds of English poems he remarks, "In the passages . . . quot-ed, there is nothing, so far as I can see, that would be considered and recognized as peculiarly English." Even more boldly René Wellek posits a "common humanity which makes every art remote in time and place . . . accessible and enjoyable to us," and insists that we have even "risen above the limitations of traditional Western taste . . . into a realm if not of absolute then of universal art." Perhaps. Again, the integrationist temper tends to ride over generic lines, not through a disinclination for or a laziness about such distinctions, but through a feeling or probing for the common ground underlying the genres, an-other kind of integer. Hence a tendency to speak of novel and drama together, to merge the kinds of fiction, to treat drama as poetry, to treat fiction as poetry, or at least to discern in each the kinds of structural relations characteristic of poetry. Hence also, I surmise, the anti-intentionalist position: it develops naturally from the view of the work as integral, from the faith in formal inner identity as against forming outer entities.

But the integrationist temper is most conspicuously evident in the sense of the wide areas of identity among discrete times, of something like a oneness of times, or at least a supratemporal unity. Hence "time-lessness" is no longer a vague, sonorous term of approbation, but a technically accurate denotation of literary substance. This is of course not a denial that differentiae exist and have meaning, but is rather a reliance upon human constants as the ultimately determining forces. These constants are the functional aspects of an integral substance. At the center are the constants of the human reality to be observed and known—the fundamental ways of action and passion and even conception. Then there are the constants of the artistic process: on the one hand, those of the forming imagination which persist centrally despite the deforming and reforming influences of changing tools and styles; on the other hand, the constants of the receptive and interpretative imagination. It is in the light of these constants that the artist and his reader both escape, not from the marks, not from the impress, of their own ages, but from bondage to and imprisonment by those ages. Membership in the era is superseded by membership in humanity. Even Taine can say of Shakespeare that "all comes from within—I mean from his soul and his genius; circumstances and externals have contributed but slightly to his development."

In tracing lightly these aspects of the differentiating and integrating activities I mean to describe rather than to debate; to be suggestive rather than magisterial, propaedeutic rather than definitive; to offer not a solvent but a perspective (upon perspectives). Hence we must avoid a rigid identification of one with Baconian "judgment" and of the other with that counterpower which has gone under various names and eventually under the Coleridgean name most appropriate to this discussion, the "esemplastic imagination"; but the analogy, as long as it does not become coercive, may be useful in a general symbolic way. Further, we stipulate that both forms of activity may be practiced by dullards or by geniuses; Shakespeare draws both on both sides. Further, the world of literary study as a whole tends to employ both perspectives simultaneously; it is customary at the same time to laud a work as "timeless" and to insist that it be seen in the light of its "times," and to mislay the perplexing theoretical problem of how the time-begotten becomes the timeless. The ideal coalescence of perspectives in one mind, however, is not frequent; it takes something of greatness to establish a fruitful mutuality between discordant habits of

In the Study

thought. Psychological security drives most of us toward, if not actually into, polar simplicities; the poles offer reassuring politics and polemics; and we will surely continue to utter, in one form or another, those ringing cross-cries of disparagement for the critical and the historical modes—"journalism" and "antiquarianism." A charming irony in these hexing clichés is their moral synonymity: each points to the same defect, an addiction to trivia and ephemeralities. By these epithets each side calls the other gossip instead of philosopher.

Each craves solidarity with the durable. Both are hostile to what is usually called "impressionistic criticism," that is, a somewhat haphazard adventure of the soul among masterpieces. (This way into literature has an appeal that, like it or not, both sides might remember. The downright scholar and the upright critic are equally in danger, as Shakespearians especially will recognize, of giving the game away to the entrepreneur with a flair for lovable gustos and disgustos, or for gustos and disgustos that seize headlines by ingenious perversity.) Each proceeds from his instinctive sense of reality to his own way of recording it, one to a demonstration by documents, the other to an analysis of organic ligaments. Demonstration has obvious ties with science; suspicious even of the great personality, it shuns all personality. How much protection the method gives against human vulnerability is perhaps arguable. Accused of inaccuracy and partisanship, Theodor Mommsen replied that "history is neither written nor made without love and hate." Arnold Stein, by no means antihistorical, remarks, "The literary historian is likely to be tempted by unawarenesses which inspire, or betray, his own insights, or even his objectivity." At any rate, against an analysis that must hope to persuade, the historian offers evidence that undertakes to prove; against a dogma of autonomy he offers the arguments of origin and consonance (the latter analogous to the regularities that in science are an alternative to cause-and-effect rationales); against a view of genius as mystery he agrees with Taine that it is a product of conditions. Troubles arise on both sides. The greater the genius, the more difficult to derive it from conditions; hence the demonstrator's temptation to the successes offered by fragmentary or peripheral problems. The greater the mystery, the larger the soul required to intuit it; because of the natural dearth of such souls, we get unilateral, tendentious, and projective critical readings of Shakespeare and many poets and novelists. The failures on each side give a great fillip to self-esteem on the other. The inadequate soul who tumbles into what has been called this-is-the-way-it-looks-to-me criticism inspires the historian to reveal the work in its objective truth, that is, in the light of the day and time that formed it.

Yet the historian himself is perhaps not home free, beyond pursuit

117

by theoretical problems. A skeptical senior historian of literature was quizzing an earnest junior historian. "You are going to describe von Tirpitz's dramas in terms of the age?" "Yes, I hope to." "You believe, then, that they are conditioned by the age?" "In some sense, yes." "You believe that the same conditioning goes on in our own age?" "In the same sense, yes." "You believe that this conditioning affects the works of the mind generally?" "Yes, I believe so." Then the quick shot from the hip: "Then you believe that the historian is conditioned by the age in which he writes?" At this the novitiate perceived the wickedness of these quasi-Socratic inquiries and quit playing. The question was deliberately oversimplifying, of course, yet it pointed to the problem of whether the literary historian himself can escape from his own matrix, of whether history itself does not become a different thing when a new point of view or a new intellectual tool becomes available, when a new atmosphere of thought, like a magnetic field, curves the rays of retrospective light. It suggests that, instead of an enduring unitary history, standing as a bulwark against an ever-moving flood of multiple criticisms—the product of so many unequal personalities—we may have also a plurality of histories, a succession of histories, begotten by minds not yet escaping from their own moment and milieu into a timeless selection and reading of the documents of time past. This would be differentiation come full circle.

Lest we forget, the approach is psychological: we are supposing different habits of mind, different human potentials, that may cohabit in or alternate in one personality, or that may prevail in different personalities. One of these instinctively asks concerning a poem or play: what are the differentiae that separate this work from before and after, and ally it distinctively with some moment in time? The other instinctive question would be: granted all the pressures of the age and its modes upon this work, what are the elements through which it transcends these impacts and becomes ultimately nontemporal? Or to revise the formulation: one personality feels something like anxiety in an open situation, scarcely more limited than human possibility, and seeks security in local habitations and names; the other is at ease in unparticularized dimensions, in uncircumscribed spaces, and, once he finds fences of local and temporal relevance installed, feels cabined, cribbed, confined. The first of these finds Flimnap insubstantial and uncomfortable until he discovers Walpole in the background; the other feels that, under the shadow of Walpole, Flimnap has seriously lost in magnitude. The first, confronted with the vast problem of Iago, instinctively tries to place Iago by consulting all the army practices that will put a hedge of ordinary actuality about him; the other will automati-

118

cally identify him with the most uncircumscribed mythic figure of evil. (A recent study does this in contemporary terms by identifying Iago with a psychoanalyst's archetypal portrait of the "vindictive man.") The two literary temperaments, as they move toward logical extremes, have respectively a reductive and an inflative function: at one extreme the work is nothing but the conventions of its day; at the other it is a vast spiritual reservoir fed by rich symbolic systems. One goes ever further into the environment, the other ever deeper into the work. One casts about for analogues, the other digs within for the anagoge. One proposes to tell what the work was, the other what it is.

What the work is: what is *is?* What the work means now? Occasionally some bold voice will say outright that the only reality of a literary work is that which may be caught in it now, with the eyes of the present; if it doesn't interest us now, it doesn't exist. Though this view is generally considered shady by both sides, it has a steady *sub rosa* life through a kind of unspoken "tolerance policy" like that of communities with antigambling laws more rigid than actual local convictions; doubtless in some way we know that we cannot make a case for whatever seems absolutely cut off from us. But the *is* of which we speak does not imply a solipsism of every hour, with the work existing only as imaged by subjectivities in continual flux. The *is* is rather that of the old grammatical description: the present tense is used for the permanently true. The integrationist mind ultimately sees this as the integer to be found beneath, and to be infinitely translatable into, the modes, the conventions, the expressive habits of the ages. The differentiating mind may challenge the existence or discoverability of this integer, and may assert the modes, conventions, and habits as final, their value simply that of the differences to be known in the endless civilizing process. There is an implicit hubris on both sides: one proposes to escape from the twentieth century into a true view of another century, another *Zeitgeist;* the other proposes to escape from the twentieth century into a true view of the timeless that in different manifestations is present to all centuries. One seeks freedom through relics that identify the ages, the other through clairvoyance into a humanity that transcends the ages. The latter does demand a most comprehensive soul, and hence of its nature it publicly betrays the critic's egotism in which the will exceeds the grasp. The sight of the work as the playground for the high-vaulting but still inelastic self understandably drives the differentiationist, the historian, into the archeological evidences which, presumably, the wilful ego cannot infect.

In theorizing that the sharply divergent premises of the debate are projections of opposing intellectual personalities, I find apparent confirmation in an entry by Camus in one of his notebooks: "The historical and the eternal mind. One has a feeling for beauty. The other for infinity." We are talking, I think, about the same human split, though the proposed dualities do not quite match. Why does the "historical" have a "feeling for beauty"? Is the common element concreteness, with its corollary of transitoriness—"Beauty that must die"? Something of the sort is implied by Camus's following note on "documents that will disappear" and so produce, in their devotees, "the reaction of hedonism and constant travel." He adds, "Here, the historical mind becomes the geographical"—an interesting sense of a unity rooted, probably, in the responsiveness to difference which I have proposed as the ground of the historical approach. The alternative "feeling for infinity" is clear—the responsiveness to the abstract, not as the insubstantial, but as what is drawn away from the concrete where mortality lies; the impulse toward the generalizing perception and in the end toward what I have called the view *sub specie aeternitatis*.

These conjectural personalities may never exist in quite pure form; I am trying to portray logical extremes, to isolate some *sine qua non*'s of each. The likely persistence of both should preclude our being locked in history, or adrift in infinity. Some crossbreeding is always evident. The integrationist shows a differentiating side by rigorous discrimination of individual works that, despite their sharing an integral substance, he calls unique; conversely the integrationist contagion will tease the historian into cyclic views that transmute the passage of things into the recurrence of things. Both individuals and the corporate profession may vacillate. But when a man can say on one page, "It is important to submit ourselves to the discipline of understanding modes of thought and feeling different from our own," and, on another, "Historical sanity requires that we also try to remember the human conditions that do not change," he is obviously determined to maintain a dual sense of literary reality—perhaps a standard aspiration in men of full consciousness. If such men do not dominate, we can perhaps expect an alternating preeminence of the differentiating and integrating habits of mind—as if by wheel of fortune, by pendular swings, or even in the manner of a "self-healing" pattern of phonemes.

We do not have much evidence to go on, however, and a qualification is in order. Though I have spoken of both perspectives as if they represent permanent habits of mind, still differentiation in time, as a formal mode of literary study, is too recent to permit a clear view of its status vis-à-vis the integrating impulse. The differentiating mode may not yet be at the top of the power that it has patently been developing in its upsurge against long dominant visions of totality. From medieval to Renaissance to Augustan thought, ideas of literature nor-

120

mally imply a oneness and permanence of truth; the aftermath of Augustan absolutism was a differentiating historicism that has been sufficiently in the ascendant to preclude, as yet, any view of pendular swings between it and ahistoric thought. It is true that the post-Augustan critics whom we remember have been implicitly anti- or at least nonhistorical; for them the literary work has been nontemporal, universal, a repository of qualities permanent and definable in general terms. The Arnoldian view of poetry as a criticism of life is in nice contrast with the Tainian view of poetry as the creature of an age; the former is an ageless voice for all ages, the latter a complex arrangement of tricky echoes requiring special adjustments of the hearing aid. But at least in the English-speaking world criticism was mainly occasional and amateur; the professional establishment, like that in France which Levin describes, was becoming an increasingly single-minded agency of differentiation. Against this background the critical movement that has had its heyday since World War I may be seen, whatever its quality, as a new and formal challenge by the integrative view; at the risk of pathetically picturing a mountainous heredity and a mousy descendant, one might regard it as an initial effort to assert and make publicly effective a sensibility that has not been in the ascendant since Augustan days. It would of course be premature to think of this as a great pendular swing, since on its account the academic welkin is rent more by knells than by peals of triumph. Recently the organic-contextual mode has been more buried than praised; yet its ghost does tend to flicker over factional battles and influence minutely the course of empire. While the vanguard of literary theory has apparently turned to other issues, the recent critical movement, so often thought heretical, has made some mark on the establishment, always hostile to unofficial visions of divine truth: the institutional residue appears in the alterations of journals and curricula, in the birth of many new journals, in changed pedagogical assumptions and practices.

Nevertheless there is a general impression that the organic-contextual school, which I have made carry the burden of the integrating temperament, has been shouldered, if not out of the temple, at least out of the sanctum. Though the old historicism may now be sharing the wealth, it is anything but dispossessed; its essential lineaments appear in a new movement that seems destined for a rich flourishing—"literature and society." Here again are the orientation to temporal context, the move away from the work as integer, and the differentiating temper that will surely transform "literature and society" into "literatures and societies." Second, there is the "new historicism," which Murray Krieger derives from Cassirer and Auerbach: in essence it treats literature as the ablest bearer of the historic vision, the best differentiator of the ages. Instead of going into the historical context to explain literature, one goes to literature to explain the historical context. For students of literature this has the advantage of making literature a thing-in-itself instead of an illustration, an echo, or a cousin of something else. Here we find an interesting ambiguity. On the one hand the main orientation is still historical: through literature one exercises the differentiating faculty and apprehends discrete eras in their separateness. Yet on the other hand if the literary imagination is the only constant power which can penetrate to the heart of the cultural complex, and to the heart of each of these as they succeed each other in time, then it partakes of the transcendent; it is not circumscribed but is in some way placed stably outside the flux which it interprets. The literary imagination does not quite become the home of the Platonic idea; we fall short of the Wildian paradox that life imitates art. Nor, in the terms of this essay, can we say that the literary imagination, as the definer of a culture, has an integrative function. But insofar as it is understood to exist independently of historical variables, we can see it as at least influenced by the integrative cast of mind. The new historicism departs from the old to the extent that it is modified, however indirectly, by the sensibility that we have attributed to the organic-contextual position.

Third, in recent years much critical energy has gone into different elaborations of the mythic view of literature, and this is customarily regarded as either an advance upon or a displacement of the organic-contextual mode. The recent preeminence of the mythic approach— the key name is of course Northrop Frye—reveals that it has recuperative power, despite intermittent attacks that might have been expected to be fatal. Like the organic-contextual mode, mythicism was a form of revolt against historicism, but it was a still earlier one. Here we must take a roundabout course by looking first at a revolution in fiction which has some illuminating parallels to the revolution in literary study. I refer to the revolt of what is usually called the psychological novel against naturalism—a metaphysical revolt in that it shifts the locus of reality from outer and tangible objects to the forming mind. In that sense it is the first denial of the primacy of circumstances, and hence of the differentiable times. It takes its stand firmly upon a mind —or at least a neurological structure—with an implicit constancy of creative function. The psychological novel is the first major move, since the abortive beginnings in Sterne, against chronological time; as the most recent student of the field puts it, "Time . . . enters the field of creative thought as something incapable of measurement and intractable to such symbolical representations as hours, days, months and

122

years." Here fiction is wrenched from its long cousinship with history: its search for a supratemporal or atemporal reality set off developments since examined in many studies of the modern fate of time. It is possible that this particular flowering in the novel in some subtle way helped make ready the air for the later critical revolt against time-oriented study. But at least there is a visible analogy between the move away from chronology in fiction, and, in literary study, the rebellion against the dominance of the historical approach.

By now the next stage of analogy will have announced itself: among the novelists moving away from environment and succession, the most notable was Joyce, and Joyce was of course the great initiator in the formal use of myth as an instrument of aesthetic order. As we shall be seeing shortly, it is more than a coincidence that one man should reject time and embrace myth. Joyce's marriage of myth is the key event in making pre–World War anthropology a supply house of literary tools. Eliot, whose *Waste Land* was still only a small voice, favorably reviewed *Ulysses* in 1923, giving credit to psychology, ethnology, and *The Golden Bough* for making admirable literary innovations possible; Yeats's *Vision* appeared in 1925; *Finnegans Wake* was coming out during the 1930s, along with the influential critical studies by Lord Raglan and Maud Bodkin. Since then the mythic perspective has steadily grown in power. In the 1960s Vivian Mercier could complain of "this Age of Anthropology" and of the "modern western intellectual, who has usually cut himself off from the myths and rituals of Judaism and Christianity, whence our western culture has drawn and continues to draw so much of its symbolism, [and who] is smitten with superstitious awe at the slightest hint of an earlier, more primitive symbolism."

In reviewing *Ulysses* Eliot said, "Instead of narrative method, we may now use the mythical method"—words which precisely sum up the notion I have been advancing of one order of art turning out another, the nonhistorical striving to supplant the historical. For the dominant view of myth, as it is put in a standard reference work, is that it "cannot possibly be history in the narrower sense, but rather the spinning-out into a tale of events which are coetaneous and eternally existent." "Not history . . . but . . . eternally existent": these terms bring us back to what is now going on in literary study, which we left momentarily for an illustrative glimpse at analogous developments in fiction. We were at the point of noting that myth criticism is sometimes considered a successor to organic-contextual criticism. What I am suggesting, on the contrary, is that, whatever the differences in theory, mythic criticism is, in its ultimate nature, a continuator in the direction taken by organic-contextual criticism; by that I mean that

123

in its search for definitions, meanings, identities, the deepest marking of mythic criticism is its atemporal or supratemporal orientation. It by-passes the differentiation of eras and cultures and instead pursues integers—onenesses, samenesses, wholes, manifestations of human nature and spirit and possibility conceived, whatever the diversity of the moldings, as eternally recurrent. If not antihistorical, it is at least nonhistorical. It carries on the strong impulse to discover, in the word *timeless*, not an effusion of sentiment, but the presence of literal meaning.

Mercier grumbled impatiently that now we can hardly discuss "any subject without introducing the notions of magic, ritual, and myth." If notions of ritual have influenced criticism less conspicuously than those of myth, they have gained an adherent in John Holloway, to whom we return for a concluding note. In *The Story of the Night* Holloway brandishes indignation at a rather inclusive group of eminent Shakespearians for treating Shakespeare unhistorically, that is, bringing into play critical concepts not available to the Elizabethan consciousness. Then, his polemics over, and other critics bleeding away in the field, Holloway proposes a completely unhistorical functioning of the tragedies: essentially they afford an experience in the rites of community, especially those of sacrifice. The "sense of community," he says, "is a major part of the consciousness of men in any society." Tragedy "does indeed elicit and awaken this side of ourselves." Shakespeare's tragedies "call forth in depth not only our sense of belonging to a community and drawing our strength from that, but also . . . of the price exacted for belonging, in the shape of constant partial self-abnegation." "They *ritualize reality*." The work is "precious . . . to society because, over centuries or over millennia, it . . . enhances . . . life." Such passages reveal plainly that in the critical use of ideas of ritual we have another evolution of the impulse to assert the timeless against the time-bound.

Such phenomena surely make the present situation, as between history and criticism, ambiguous. The energetic attack of criticism upon history that broke out some years back has subsided; in turn this aggressive critical movement has fallen under the shadow of the new historicism, and critical energy has shifted from the autotelic text to the myth-bearing or myth-making text and occasionally to the ritualizing text. This much is clear. Yet the new historicism appears to be subtly influenced by, and mythicism is an evident reassertion and enlargement of, the integrative impulse which I have proposed is the heart of the original critical revolt. Hence two statements by Leone Vivante will surely seem less reckless and heretical now than they would have seemed earlier. "The concept of an *active* principle, not entirely derivable from its conditions, . . . reveals and develops itself in poetry in a supremely genuine and direct way." "The feeling of the intrinsic and eternal character of thought's and life's inward values and modes, as prevailing over the historical transitory interests and the particular ends and objects, belongs to the essence of art." Yet—and these *yet*'s mark the ambiguity—the differentiating cast of mind seems so strong in the general intellectual life of our age that it is easily possible to imagine, in future literary studies, an intensified historicism and an unlimited expansion of the concept of derivability. That was the expectation of the young man who argued that history had not yet really been tried.

The integrating and differentiating activities may be constants of the soul or special flowerings of a modern psyche still short of dissolution; or the conflicts we have sketched may precede a long triumph of the differentiating perspective that seems generally more characteristic of us. When the differentiating activity becomes a center of faith as well as a way of thought, it produces some odd nonliterary attacks on criticism. The organic-contextual mode has been called "reactionary," as if its literary doctrines were only a facade for social and political Jacobitism. Such polemics come out of confusion and out of the doctrine that literature, since it has social origins, must directly serve social ends; hence to the adherent of such a doctrine the denial of an immediate social relevance in art seems a wickedness that deserves strong words. But to leave polemics behind and look at the situation with a neutral analytic eye: there is indeed a kinship between modes of literary study and general ways of conceiving reality. The nonhistorical, integrative sensibility in criticism has some affinity with what, in an attempt to find a single term of wide suggestive value, I will call the religious sensibility: the sense of the organic, and of the reality which lies outside time; the impulse to identify constants, the overarching truth, the enduring integer, and so to attribute, to change and progress, a large measure of the illusive. On the other hand, the historical, differentiating temper in literary study has an affinity with the inclusive vision of truth as pluralistic, relative, nonhierarchical, successive in time, variable in space. I am describing two extremes which, presumably, ought to modify each other and be brought together in an ideal fusion. But if I am correct that the pluralistic-variable bias is dominant in modern thought, then literary history seems to have a lusty future, whatever the revisionist strength of the organic-contextual mode, of mythicism in its different styles, and now, if Holloway's espousal is persuasive, of what may come to be called the new ritualism.

125

We have tried to emphasize, not glories and failings, nor a division of territory among imperial powers, but the intellectual, and behind it the psychological, structure of two approaches to literature. Hence the view of history as a dialogue among persons of the differentiating habit of mind, and of criticism as a dialogue among persons of the integrating habit of mind. Both dialogues are inconclusive. They may try to talk each other down, but again they may be overheard by each other. The persistence of the critical dialogue is likely to push the historical dialogue back toward the work instead of letting it stay content among the palaeological remains. The persistence of the historical dialogue must act as a brake on the excesses of the unitary vision, on wilfulnesses, on those adventures among masterpieces which are experienced not by the perceptive many-sided soul but by the unicellular ego in need of triumph. On rare occasions we find one man participating in both dialogues and for a luminous moment uniting them — Granville-Barker on Shakespeare, Ellmann on Joyce, Wellek on criticism. Neither dialogue holds back the inspired monologist who, on whichever side, escapes the inconclusiveness that limits the many: a historian like Kittredge, or a critic whose eye for the timeless is confirmed, as only it can be, by his surviving his own times. Here I think most easily of Johnson on Shakespeare.

AT THE BOTTOM OF EVERYTHING:
EVERYTHING:
HUMANITIES

12
Outside the Laws
The Humanities versus the Sciences

Humanities and sciences: old terms—old concepts—and so even old stuff, familiar enough to all. But are they really? Try asking academics themselves: how many can say much more about these terms than that they denote different areas of study that always bunk together in the college catalogue? How do any of us really distinguish them? Why are we "for" one or another?

In one sense, these terms suffer from underdefinition and overuse. All abstract terms in wide use get to resemble clothes worn too steadily —spread, seamstretched, baggy. They have to be ironed, blocked, reshaped periodically. So *humanities* and *sciences* can use at least some freshening up, creasing, pressing: they can be made to hang a little straighter.

The two can best be worked on together, if only because, like coats and trousers, they are usually thought of together. And if they are not always clearly distinguished (for they are cut from the same cloth), at least it is rarely forgotten that they have somewhat different functions. In trying to separate these functions as sharply as possible, I will give greater space and emphasis to the humanities, partly because they are my home territory, but more because they are in much worse shape semantically. *Sciences* at least means experiments, laboratories, marvels; *humanities* hardly means anything more definite than books, "olden times," and inadequate regard for the profit motive.

In talking more about one, and in using the other mainly for illustration, there is a danger. It is the danger of seeming guilty of salesmanship—that play for the buyer's favor that makes free with the nature of things (by embellishing or concealing) and makes hay with the nature of persons (by teasing, tempting, and pushing). To some readers it may seem odd that, in a simple effort to define the humanities, one may be afraid of looking like a salesman. The fear will seem less pointless to readers who know the inside of some of our academic department stores, where there is a real play for the customer's "education dollar." This play is not found in all institutions or in all fields; it breaks out mostly in nouveau riche or social-climbing fields that play for popularity first and hope to reap respectability later.

Many a staff member is, in effect, a pitchman. But he is not so much raucous as insinuating. Take a good look at our setup, he whispers. The courses are not too hard. No strain on the brain. We are very democratic. Friendly atmosphere. Special clubs for majors. Greek letter patent pending. Grading reasonable. Last year a surprising number of our majors made Phi Beta Kappa. We are a growing concern. All our products move quickly in government and business. Now we are making big inroads in the high-school field; this will open up thousands of new jobs. Have you seen our latest major requirements? Positively no math, no sciences, no foreign languages required. Now you can take up to 80 percent of all your credits right in our own department. This keeps you on the beam and avoids confusion. Don't miss this opportunity. Sign now—but hold it! Special bulletin! We are now considering a new bargain rate by which you can trade in your old high-school credits for up to thirty hours of brand-new advanced placement credit! And another bargain in the latest fashion: we are arranging a number of courses (maximum enrollment 750) in which you can grade yourself! And still as a super-added absolutely-no-charge premium, we have added to the staff three (3) Relevance Advisers who have studied the whole university catalogue to tell you personally which courses are with it and will help you get with it! (All our courses are relevant, but yes; all our basic principles are post-1965.) But there is still one additional goodie for our deserving students: we now conduct most courses on the group therapy principle, and in a few easy lessons you teach yourself health while you teach yourself our great field!

This kind of grab for the customer's dollar, and for the favor from which dean's dollars flow, exists in part because both customers and the management think of a campus as a medley of bargain basement, clinic, and visa office for everybody making the journey of Life. A good number of outsiders and insiders think of education as a form of unemployment insurance or health insurance or as baptism and confirmation in a new spiritual kingdom. They want a warranty label which says in effect, "This product inspected by registrar's office and certified to meet minimum production standards. Transferred to distribution agencies for labor market, white-collar division," or "This product certified to have got well and to have privileges of thinking well of himself," or "This product trained in recognizing the evils of the world and in quick ways of putting them down." So we get ready to affix the labels.

The humanities and sciences cannot say too often that their business is not with vocational education or even with the kind of professional education that puts some strain on the brain or with psychotherapy or with the production of secular evangelists ready to battle with vice, and drive it out, and thus produce the Eden we all deserve. Though they may teach him, their main job is not with the man who studies economics in order to be an investments counselor, or art in order to be a commercial designer, or even with the man who studies English in order to be an editor or science in order to be an engineer or doctor. Rather their chief function is with people who want to grow up intellectually, and they must try to persuade students to seek ends that can't be labeled at all: to know more and to see more clearly than when they started, to have the mind of an adult rather than that of an adolescent, a trained dog, a slave, or even an overseer of slaves. (Granted, the two courses may, on rare occasions, overlap: a searcher for knowledge may find that he has come up with useful skills, and a seeker of gainful employment may find knowledge that will help him grow up as well as grow fat.) The humanities and sciences are seeking to humanize the higher animal—to get him out of the zoo and stop him short of the opposite mantrap of mechanization. They have rather a task, for zoo and push-button life are cousins: the zoo is a built-in, premental automation, and automation is a sort of man-made zoo life. Hence it is shockingly easy for man, when he has climbed out of one row of wire cages, to climb contentedly into another row of wired containers, wired indeed for practically everything, or, in a later phase of impatience, to grow homesick for the original zoo (or a prezoo zoicism) and to decide that the best way to restore its felicity is to wire up devices for eliminating everything else that depends on wires.

Somewhere between these no-thought extremes of pure animal instinct and pure switchboard plug-in systems is the life of adult human intelligence. A lucky few may achieve it without benefit of college education, and many may take college courses for years and, alas, get not one whit nearer to it. When education does help, it encourages two processes of mind: knowing more and thinking better. It works principally through two great approaches to truth in which both thought and imagination are working with utmost freedom—the sciences and the humanities. We should remember that these serve the same general end. But they go about it differently.

In the sciences—natural, biological, social—the procedure is to discover and formulate general laws: laws about the behavior of all kinds of entities from invisible impulses and submicroscopic particles to large organs and organisms and masses of land and air, from the human body and mind to social bodies, from minorities to nations. So we have the laws of aerodynamics or Gresham's law or the laws of supply and demand or even Parkinson's law (a joke which came true), or the lawlike principles implied in such everyday terms as repression, overcompensation, balanced diet, status, inflation, diminishing returns, counterrevolution. Laws may change or be amended; there may be troubling contradictions or exceptions or problems of jurisdiction; instead of absolute laws, there may be other kinds of regularity which we call probabilities or correspondences. But there is always present the idea of the rule, of the regular sequence or relationship of phenomena, of the quantitative norm or the defining curve according to which all individual cases, or experience in general, may be interpreted.

The humanities work differently. (I shall refer principally to literature, though remembering that the arts have much in common with it, and that in college catalogues philosophy and history often share quarters with it.) They are not concerned with discovering and formulating laws. These are the field of the great individual insight, thought, and creative imagination.

There are of course brilliant individual work and creativity in the sciences, too. But we must observe two distinguishing facts. The first is that in all of the sciences a characteristic procedure is research by a research team, whose members subordinate their individuality to the common objective; whereas in literature, the arts, and philosophy—and even to some extent in history—systematic work by a team is virtually impossible. In these the individual goes it alone. The second point is that in science what the brilliant individual does is discover a new law; it becomes a part of the system of thought by which all other investigators in the field are bound. In the humanities the brilliant individual creates in a new way or creates a new thing, has a new idea about the good or the true or the beautiful, or a new idea about the meaning of the Renaissance or the so-called westward movement of civilization or the American frontier; we may call this an inspiration, or an insight, or a brilliant conjecture, or an act of creation, or a fascinating theory, but we never, never think of it as a law, or as in any way binding on other humanists. The greater this new thing is, the more attention it will seize, the more faith it will arouse; but in a purely technical sense everyone, literally everyone, is free to laugh at

132

it, resist it, hate it, or act as if it did not exist. Anyone can say about it, "This is one man's opinion," and let it go at that.

Let us put it this way. If a research laboratory discovers a new law of metal fatigue in airplane wings, that law is binding on all designers and manufacturers of airplanes. But if a great artist works out a new kind of decorative design for the interior of a plane, or a great fiction writer writes a brilliant new story that is distributed for reading material to plane travelers, or if an imaginative and creative airplane pilot, such as St. Exupéry, writes poetically about flight and treats it as a kind of philosophical and spiritual experience—everyone, literally everyone, is free to disregard utterly the artist, the novelist, and the poetical pilot. Everyone is free to yawn, to disbelieve, or to set up opposition views of beautiful design or of the world presented by novelist and poet. The fact is, of course, that artist, novelist, and poet get plenty of attention, respect, and even belief—more, sometimes, than they can sustain. But not because they can ever assert or intimate that they have got hold of a law whose truth only a madman would deny.

In other words: science proves, the humanities persuade. One offers rational argument, the other calls on faith. Science works from evidence, experimental or statistical, that apparently forces a conclusion; the humanities are created by a gifted man's hunch or dream or even fantasy. Science aspires to rigid impersonality; the humanities exist because of an extraordinary person's sense of truth. We do not respond to his evidence, his proof, or his powers of reason, but to the sweep, the depth, the power of his individual grasp of things; to the personal knowledge and sensitivity that he shows; in a word, to the complex sum of factors that we call personality. In his impersonal passive voice the scientist says, "It has been demonstrated that this is how things are." The humanist or artist says, "This is the way *I* see it." Finally, by virtue of its laws, science can be predictive: we know how much rainfall there will be, where planes will wear out, how radiation will affect the germ plasm, how many murders there will be per million of population, how many persons will die of leukemia, when eclipses will occur, what conditions will produce delinquent youth, when and where artificial satellites will be visible. The humanities and arts do not essay the prediction of things to come, Each work simply says, "This is the way man looks to me now. This is the way things look now. This is the way they feel now."

In summary. Science wants to establish laws. Writers and artists are essentially indifferent to the principle of law; occasionally they may feel that to be truthful they have to run counter to law—that is, to accepted rules of society and art. Philosophy, at least in its present dominant practices, will try to get behind both attitudes by asking what we mean by law. History, which by definition looks backward, is always tempted in a small part of its soul (and rather to the disgruntlement of the rest of its soul) to try also to look forward, to formulate laws that will give us, for social and political organisms existing in time, some of the certainty that we have about climate, celestial action, and old age. There are too many variables, and the various theories of history are less like laws than works of art—not proved, not binding, not passed by the legislatures of the intellectual world, but wonderfully suggestive, giving us imaginative clues to events in sequence, a hypothesis of the course of events which has its uses. History balances precariously between science and humanities, bonded to tell what did happen, longing to tell what must happen, dedicated to demolishing dreams about the past, but now and then slipping into prophecy about the future.

The humanities, it may seem, have not much of a leg left to stand on. They give no laws; rather they stand outside the laws and say only, "This is the way I see it." What claims do these private views, these outlaw assertions, have upon us? What they have, in the end, is the authority of a certain truthfulness that we cannot resist. It is almost twenty-five hundred years since the Greek dramatists wrote plays that we can still regard as fresh revelations of human truth; we can apply our newest psychological insights to the characters, and find them in these latest terms consistent and meaningful. If the humanities are not predictive, nevertheless they can present the constants of human nature so sharply that they will be good for indefinite futures. About the same time that Harvey was demonstrating the circulation of the blood, Shakespeare was inventing lines for an imaginary prince, Hamlet; about the same time that Newton was formulating the law of gravity, Milton was inventing fantastic deeds for a mythological demon, Satan. In some way Hamlet and Satan, these imaginary beings, seem no less real or true or meaningful, and therefore have no less power over us, than the demonstrated laws of Harvey and Newton. They are the creation, not of any chance person who wants an audience (as we all do), but of extraordinary individuals who in some way, really a mysterious way, see more than the rest of us, see more widely, more deeply, more freshly. There is no substitute for the gifted individual's sense of life, his sense of the world we see and feel, of human nature and conduct, of all immediate actualities and of truths that seem to lie beyond them. The essence of individuality is penetration and creativity. The humanities are the sum total of the work of remarkably gifted individuals who look directly at the world and at life, endow them with a unique

134

shape and color, and yet through this unique form give us a new sense of insight into reality. Hence we traditionally speak of them in images of creation and images of seeing—such as insight, vision, and revelation. These are ways of defining the extralegal voice.

The literary artist may see in many different ways. He may envisage the human scene in terms of its great breadth and variety—as do Chaucer, Shakespeare, Dickens, Tolstoi, or Thomas Mann. He may see human reality in outright fantastic terms—as do Swift in *Gulliver's Travels* and Kafka in his tales and Duerrenmatt and Frisch in their dramas. He may seem to be fantastic because he sees so much of man's contradictory depths—as does Dostoevsky. He may see man's inner inconsistencies and self-deceptions as morally significant but as laughable—as do Molière and Jane Austen, or as the object of contempt, as do Boccaccio and Byron. He may see the disastrous conflict of idea and impulse, as does Ibsen, or of aspiration and impulse, as does Sophocles. He may see the ideal as both silly and noble, and the practical as both sensible and petty—as does Cervantes. He may see the ironic way in which our moral energy misfires and is misdirected—as does Joseph Conrad. He may look with great intenseness at all the vices that man can practice, and at all the excellences of which he is capable, and arrange these in a kind of rank order—as does Dante. He may look at the problem of good and evil in terms of a strange, vast, exotic myth—as do Milton and Goethe, or in terms of the interaction between men and institutions, as does Hardy, or in terms of the choices that men make because of a deep inner blindness or perceptiveness, as does Henry James, or in terms of situations on the borderline between daily life and obsessive dream as does Melville. The writer may peer as solemnly as a surveyor (like a naturalistic novelist), burst into the wild glare of a prophet, like D. H. Lawrence, or assume a frivolous giddiness, in the manner of various comic writers from Laurence Sterne to Ronald Firbank. He may catch the momentary quirk, the flash of lust or hate, the curious thought, the subtle despair, the surprising resemblance, the destructive passion, the seductive dream, the heavy or witty disillusionment, the troubling or sustaining faith—the endless range of moods, passions, beliefs, and thoughts that are the material of the lyric poets, from Wyatt and Donne and Dryden to Keats and Hopkins and Eliot.

So much for concrete examples of what the humanities are about. In them we get a picture of human life from innumerable points of view. These views are highly personal; in that sense they are the opposite of impersonal scientific law. (It is because of the individuality of the work that we habitually call it "unique": not unusual, not "different," but "one of a kind.") But this preeminence of the personal does not mean

135

that the writer or artist or imaginative thinker is free to run off into a one-man world of fantasies, like a devotee of pot and speed. On the contrary, he bears a great weight of responsibility: his vision is of a general truth of the world, and he must labor to validate it. Though he is less than, and different from, a research team, he actually takes on a larger subject than any research team would dream of: his subject is all of mankind, or, in other terms, the whole personality of man. There are two main ways in which his material differs from the material of the scientist who is in search of laws. The literary artist must present every eccentricity, every deviation, every perversity of which man is capable—that is, every kind of character and action that seems to fall *outside* of general law—and must try to see its human significance, as does Shakespeare with Iago, and Melville with Captain Ahab, and Dostoevsky with Raskolnikov and Stavrogin. But at the same time he is aiming, must aim, at a kind of totality, or wholeness of picture, that goes *beyond* law. His subject is a human nature which, though many laws are operating within it, is not as a whole thing definable by law. It must be approached by intuition rather than by formulae. The work of literature is always to try to grasp, to present, to re-present that whole—a whole which in one sense is the sum of all the differing in-dividuals that constitute humanity, and which in another sense is the sum of all the divergent forces, needs, and choices that constitute a representative human being. The humanities try to create a sense of what being human is like, not of human life broken down into parts that can be studied in laboratory or computer and seen as the mechani-cal operation of laws, but in the total organism, where everything is going at once. Why is Hamlet interpreted in so many ways? Because. as a recent critic argues, all the other critics are silly, and don't really look at the text? Perhaps. More likely, I think, because Shakespeare got so much of human reality into Hamlet that a reader has a hard time getting it all into one picture; hence different readers honestly see quite different Hamlets and come up with excellent evidence for their varying interpretations.

This large picture of the human whole is not, like a scientific conclu-sion, verifiable. We cannot run experiments or computations, or apply it under controlled conditions, and thus be assured that it is true. Yet in a sense it can be verified: it is verified by posterity. It lives because for generation after generation it is found to correspond to something actual in the human being. It gives man something like knowledge. It is not the knowledge offered by laws, formulae, and propositions. It is rather like the knowledge which comes out of experience itself. But it happens that experience itself does not offer us a very large quantity of knowledge. Each person's experience is too restricted; it comes too slowly; we are too close to it to have perspective; the significant elements are too mixed up with routine, details, and ordinary confusion. If science is the world of law, experience in general may be said to be lawless. Somewhere in between are the humanities—outside the law, but trying to bring lawless experience into line, or at least into the line of vision. They are concerned with more inclusive, more disorderly, less manageable chunks of reality than is science, and yet to these chunks they set limits, give a form, and provide a perspective that we don't find in pure experience, which is a mixed-up and unruly affair. I am here setting up an imaginary diagram—a line connecting two distant extremes. At one extreme is all of life as we experience it; here it is hard to see order and meaning. At the other extreme is science: here we get order and meaning by cutting life down into separate parts that can be defined by law. Somewhere between the two extremes are the humanities, which try to deal with life as a whole, not cutting it down to certain measurable ingredients, but still giving it a form and meaning that are difficult to find when one is in the middle of life itself.

Let us take an example. Suppose you are a young woman, one of three daughters, devoted to your old father, but troubled by his instability and tempestuousness. Suddenly he demands the most outrageous flattery. You go as far as you can without being humiliated, but it isn't far enough. He is insanely angry, divides up all his property between your two sisters, quarrels with friends who object to this, tries to cut off your suitors. The only one left is a Russian; so, utterly cut off from family and country, off you go to Russia. Your sisters fight your father; their followers are drawn in, and since they are all in politics, the family violence breaks out into civil war. Then you get back, but only as an enemy; you are reunited with your father, now penitent, but driven temporarily out of his mind by his anguish; then you are captured by the gangster types that are doing the dirty work for your sisters, and murdered. Even if one survived these events—obviously, with a modernized detail or two, the story of Cordelia in *King Lear*—they could hardly add up to more than a meaningless morass of intolerable suffering and horror. Inside the actual experience one could only be dazed or crushed by the wild medley of destructive events. But the play takes those events and, without reducing our sense of their actuality, molds them into a form which makes it possible for us to look at them from some distance, to contemplate them, and thus to have some sense of being above them and comprehending them. I am trying to illustrate the almost magical way in which the humanities give intelligible form to chaotic human experience without refining it down to the abstractions and formulae that science works with.

And yet this is only half of it. For in this literary experience there is an extraordinary contradiction, and this contradiction is the heart of it. On the one hand, we have seen, the literary work takes us outside the actual happenings, and in this respect it is somewhat like a scientific formula or law. But the formula or law places us irrevocably outside full human experience, while the drama or novel, on the other hand, also puts us back into the experience as participants. We are both outside and inside, both observers and actors. This is the mystery of literary art. We are in the experience, of course, not as actual participants, but as imaginative participants. But this kind of insideness is a very real thing, so real that adult readers often find the literary experience too painful to endure, as though actuality itself were harming them.

Now the important thing is that imaginative participation opens up for us a range of experience that is usually denied to us in actuality. What I am getting at is this: in presenting human actuality to us, the human ties really work in two opposite ways. In one direction, we have seen, they organize experience for us—that is, cut it down, give it a definite beginning and ending, bound it, do away with some of the mess and disorganization of daily life. In the other direction they expand and enlarge experience for us by making available to us, by bringing us into, many kinds of action, feeling, and thought that our ordinary lives might not open up to us at all, though in a sense these are natural to us and to all of human life. For we may as well face it: most of us do lead relatively narrow lives, compared with the great reaches of experience that are in the human potential; we exercise only small parts of the human nature with which we are endowed. For instance, we rarely become great lovers. We do not commit murder. We do not become martyrs, or have mystical visions, or make fantastic voyages, or fall into insoluble conflicts of passion. We do not get very close to the great thoughts, the great wrongdoings, or the great acts of love and charity that are potentially ours as human beings. But the humanities induct us into all of these depths. In some way they let us expand into humanity in its full scale of possibilities, evil as well as good.

This experience works in different ways. Insofar as it provides an exercise of human potentialities, it ought to be a good thing in itself: it counteracts the danger of simply being idle, static, shut in. In this sense it offers us a kind of action. But at the same time this action is a means of knowledge: from the very feeling of roles that our daily life is not likely to provide we get to know something of what we as human beings are like.

This is the kind of knowledge that ought to contribute to wisdom. Wisdom is an ultimate virtue of humanity, but it is a virtue that nowadays we do not often speak of, even when speaking of it would be appropriate. Not long ago I read a batch of student themes in which the writers were explaining why they attended a university. What were their dreams and ideals? In the main hardly more than something called "success"—that is, getting on in the world, getting ahead of others, getting more things, and not having to work too hard for them (and for some, of course, that other kind of "success"—the moral triumph of at last putting a stop to the evils that man has practiced and endured for so long). In this view the distinguished scientists, artists, critics, writers, and intellectuals who constitute a university are asked to give the young a few steers on how to keep up with, or get ahead of, the Joneses in subsistence or status (or to get ahead of "successful" people by punishing them or putting them down because "success" embodies an antihuman vice). In my sample there was not one word of desire for learning, for excellence of mind, or for wisdom.

Occasionally there is a good sign. There is the amusing joker who a few years ago sued his university for fraudulent practices because it had failed to teach him wisdom (though now the business of bringing suits is in itself hampering the proper activities of the university). There is the fact that we use "wise guy" as a term of disparagement: we distinguish between trickiness and real quality of mind. But some of our terms of praise are less reassuring. Take the term "the open mind." This may denote some real virtues. But often it describes a structure characterized less by light than by draughtiness, and by the clatter of so many things blowing through that few things are ever kept in place. Again, we hear a man praised because he "has a mind like a steel trap." This is a rather frightening substitute for wisdom. It gives a picture of a sawtooth type lying in wait for victims, snapping mechanically on to them, and then hanging rigidly on until stopped by force; indeed, it takes a crowbar to get this monstrous machine open again. The steel-trap type, I suspect, is only the wise guy who has got a commission (or tenure). Then there is the "modern mind": it gives a mastery of every other man's untruth—by means of whatever tight doctrine discovers all men's illusions but those of the doctrinaire himself.

No, wisdom is neither something so open that it is always coming apart, nor so closed that it shuts everything in or out, nor so modern as to be routinely skeptical in all directions but one. Let us now try being affirmative: the true mark of wisdom is knowing, at the same time, how man does act, how he can act, and how he should act. If we do not know enough of now man does act and will act, we are likely to be only censorious or sentimental. If we know only how man does act, we become hopeless or cynical. To be either sentimental and reformist, or cynical and escapist, is usually the product of knowing too little of human nature, of its immense range of possibilities, from the destructive to the creative, from the depraved to the saintly (the nineteenth century had too easy an eye for the saintly; in reaction, the twentieth century has resolved never to be outdone in its singleminded vision of the depraved). It is that infinite range of possibilities which is the material of the humanities. In them we see humanity, and hence ourselves. Self-knowledge has always been thought a high mark of wisdom.

In no sense do I intend to exclude the large realm of the sciences from the sources of wisdom. I have wanted only to suggest the kinds of knowledge that sciences and humanities contribute toward the mature understanding, the human excellence, that we call wisdom. Hence I have tried to distinguish what we learn through formulae and laws, through controlled evidence and proof, from what we learn through nonlegal, unproved, unprovable visions of human reality that have the authority, not of logic, but of individual insight and of the assent that we continue to give them as one age after another goes by. We need all we can get of both—of the laws and of the humanities that lie outside the laws. The latter are outside the laws because they have to be, for they seek meaning, at one extreme, in the individual experience that may seem to be sheer idiosyncrasy, to come under no law at all; and, at the other extreme, in the totality that is too manifold to be expressed usefully in the form of law. And at either extreme the humanities are concerned with human beings struggling in a basic realm that has nothing to do with law—with choices, values, the puzzle of good and evil, of impulse and obligation, of self and nonself.

This outlaw knowledge is indispensable, yet the humanist who sets out to discover it, form it, and present it has set himself a large task. The life of the outlaw is never easy; if he acts in the realms of knowledge, he has the difficulty of convincing an age that has especial veneration for knowledge by laws. He cannot even pose as a Robin Hood, a sentimentally pleasing outlaw who takes it from the rich and gives it to the poor. No, he takes it from two places—from himself and from everybody; then he gives it back to everybody, in a new form. All we have to do is to take it.

13
Humanisticism
and Melodrama
Styles in Combat

The words of my title may not, at first glance, be altogether clear in meaning. But even in initial fuzziness they are not entirely equivalent. *Melodrama* is an old word, but *humanisticism* is, to the best of my knowledge, a new one. Its slick ungainliness (if any *ism* word is ungainly in these ismatic days) may give some clue to the idea I mean it to convey. But let that conveyance be, for the moment, indirect. Let *humanisticism* lie there, like an unetherized patient upon the examination table, until we are ready to come back and see what makes it a patient. Let identification be postponed, as in a detective story, until we have surrounded the central character with a context of evidence— some, of course, misleading, some farfetched, but all intended to spur the defining imagination. The inner culprit, if there is one, will appear in time (diagnosis and detection are, after all, much the same).

Melodrama, of course, sounds like a culprit *ab initio*. But, like any other character that sometimes falls short of good citizenship in the republic of letters, it reveals itself in a number of different guises. To avoid an excess of mystery, we need to pin it down. For our purposes, melodrama is a way of looking at life. In essence it attributes whatever is wrong to evil men, and its faith is that good men can decontaminate or eliminate evil men and thus restore, more or less permanently, a normal state of basic well-being. In melodrama the split is between good men and evil men, not between good and evil in man. It is the world of the popular theater, where we are healed of self-doubt and purged of any sense of wrongdoing. On that stage we are victors without guilt.

We like to extend that stage as far as it will go out into daily actuality. War is all melodrama; so is politics. In government, and even in

141

business and professional life, we find it easy to measure time by evils
that thwart us and by enemies put down. This goes on with equal
vigor where perhaps one might not expect it—among philosophers,
artists, intellectuals generally, who have often the sense of protecting
little Edens against serpentine invaders bent upon destroying excellence of mind and soul. It is a role that leads rather easily to self-congratulation, and to making public claims for the powers and merits of
one's domain.

This happens in the humanities too. In "Outside the Laws: The Humanities" I tried to say what the humanities are good for, but I also
tried to protect myself against sounding like a salesman. Many of us in
the humanities tend to raise our voices in a defensive and promotional
way. Ever since World War II we have been protesting the value of
our services to the community. Whatever the real virtues of the humanities, we do not sound quite right when we seize bullhorns and
loudly proclaim the salvationary powers of our enterprise. What purports to be a disinterested pursuit of grace of mind begins to look like
a strengthening of organizational prerogatives, a membership drive
for a quasi-ecclesiastical body claiming influence at the gates of a cultural heaven. We should not be surprised if some rude auditor retorted,
"Physician, save thyself." For we should have to acknowledge that
from an assemblage of scholars, critics, and poets one could collect
enough moral and spiritual clay feet to supply handsomely a ceramic
factory for the making of grotesque figurines. Yet here it is necessary
to avoid what may be called the Fallacy of the Imperfect Minister: the
vulgar supposition that the flaw in the priest establishes the hollowness
of the creed. It is the nature of creeds to envisage goals that strain the
talents of the ministers. Nevertheless promotionalism fixes attention
upon the promoter; and if he claims publicly to have the keys to ur-
banity, largeness of mind, imaginative insight, and wisdom, he may
anticipate exacting inspection, and perhaps blunt inquiry.

During the emotional spasms of the immediate postsputnik period I
was rather relieved to be abroad on sabbatical leave and hence beyond
the clutches of an earnest colleague who was collecting signatures to a
manifesto inveighing against the new emphasis on the study of science
and warning everybody to keep eyes properly fixed on the humanities,
where true safety lies. Beyond my perhaps finicky distaste for this
hawking of our wares lay a vague sense that the whole project, though
it might be high-minded, was wrong-headed. Yet at the same time I
was a little concerned to find myself unconcerned, happily out of it;
was I ducking responsibility, just going along for the professional ride
while others fought for space on the road? That is the kind of question

142

which no man can answer in his own favor with final assurance, but I found no weakening of my sense that this we're-as-important-as-science petition was misconceived. It was a misdirection of energies, a misidentification of what we call "the enemy." The old melodrama of the good humanities versus the bad sciences is not the archetype latent in the specific plot in which we must all act. There *is* an "enemy," and we must dread it because it is hostile to both humanities and sciences; I am convinced that science and we have more to ally us than to separate us. At first blush this may look like a severe case of cryptoscientism. If need be, I shall have to risk seeming like a secret agent of the cyclotron party until eventually I reveal what I see as the structure of the melodrama in which scientist and humanist, far from being antagonists, share the role of the beleaguered hero.

I want to get at this, indirectly for a time, by glancing at two other melodramas that I think have hidden affiliations with the ill-constructed humanities-sciences melodrama. The first of these is the perennial old age-versus-youth melodrama in its recent phases, and if this seems an alien topic, I am content to let it seem so for now. The old antagonism had an almost incredibly novel form in the 1950s and early 1960s; then in the later 1960s it reverted to its traditional format, albeit with an intensity that threatened stability and even peace (and perhaps may still do so). In this traditional format, age accuses youth of ignorance of reality, while youth accuses age of ignorance of the good and the true. This is expectable; the danger of experience is corruption, and the danger of inexperience is the confusion of fact and dream. Ordinarily the two dangers don't do much more than grumble at each other. Things begin to get out of hand only when visionary youth falls into the hands of calculating demagogues who promise to force corruption out of existence and force virtue into the saddle now. This is very frightening, and age has shown its fright by an incoherent medley of *peccavi*'s, flattery, bribery, surrender, condemnation, counterviolence, and the most bitter denunciation ever launched by greybeards against beards. But, I repeat, this is in the main an intensification of standard operating procedure, and so it is of less concern in the present discourse. What is extraordinarily interesting about it, however, is that in a very real sense we elders asked for the kind of attack we received in the late 1960s. At least we prepared the way for it; we may well have brought it on. For this new outbreak of the old ring-out-the-old-ring-in-the-new melodrama directly reverses what went on in the 1950s. Then it was we elders who leaped to the attack (and in our blindness we still keep repeating the old slurs that at last were followed by the reaction which has scared us half to death). This is what I have called the "almost incredibly novel form" of the old melodrama in the 1950s. We need to look back at what we started then, and see if we can learn something from it.

Normally we in the camp of age accuse youth of adolescence; in the 1950s we accused it of old age. Our traditional case against youth is that it is so unlike us; in the 1950s the charge was that youth was so like us. But here I am not accurate, for we were not even content to be like ourselves; we berated our juniors for not being so young as we were or thought we were. We were angry young men energetically castigating our tired old sons, attacking our junior elders, for not conforming to our own virile nonconformity. We ex-bohemians of the twenties and ex-revolutionaries of the thirties abused the veterans of the forties and the multiple fathers of the fifties for pursuing reality by different routes which we supposed to be less spirited and disorderly than our own, and therefore less noble and manly. By now we can already see, in our style of those days, unfortunate reminiscences of the complacent Mr. Dedalus, smirkingly assured that as a lustier flouter of official rules, a sampler of wine and wench, he is more of "a man" than young Stephen.

Various motives may have stirred this original critique of the youth of the fifties (a critique which is still a cliché in our own day, though subsequent events ought to have put it out of business). Ex-youths all have lost youths to justify, and regretting the failures of others is a standard brand of self-justification. Or imputing to others a lamentable flight to safety may be a relatively safe way of intimating that if our own exteriors are placid, nevertheless our interiors are a turmoil of volcanic thoughts. If we suspect that we have left the pursuit of danger behind us, the damning of others for the same retreat may at once cast a veil over our own derelictions and administer a little vicarious self-flagellation. (I recall the case of a free-lance critic who, on becoming a professor some years ago, unleashed the most biting blasts at professors for being safe and stodgy: surely an oblique self-punishment and yet a way of claiming meritorious exemption from the usual occupational hazards.) Or if one has not grown up—and I must admit to suspecting some of the attackers of youth of this slip—one is not pleased by something that looks like maturity; so one naturally calls it premature senility. And I spotted one case in which Professor A, was offended by the docility of academic youth because youth did not revolt against the unfortunate positions of Professor B. We rarely attack our own followers for docility, or decry their lack of intellectual boldness if they do not dissent against our dogmatic dissents. In fact youth most charmingly proves his critical freedom by assenting to our dissent.
144

But the excavation of underground motives does not of itself under-
mine the position; contrary to the working principles of most polemics, selfish, indeed loathsome motives may lie behind shrewd or
even devastating analyses, analyses that have to be met in other ways
than by denouncing the messiness or the malice, the self-deception or
self-protection, of the analyst. So the silliness of middle-aged knights
once errant is not the issue. What is the issue is the mistakenness of
their detraction. I felt it mistaken at the time. This cannot be a claim to
early insight into a generally accepted truth, for the detraction of the
tired and passive students of the fifties, as we have noted, still goes on.

In the indictment of youth for failure to be sufficiently reckless navi-
gators what is most hair-raising is the implied theory of reality: I
mean the pernicious metaphysics which equates the pursuit of freedom
and truth with the habitual practice of dissent. Yes, I recognize the
hygienic values of dissent and denial, the necessity of negation in the
pursuit of freedom, and the considerable problem of getting our society to be at ease with dissent; and I do not propose to butter up the
like-mother-used-to-make conservationists. In fact I am equally dis-
turbed by the camp that would eliminate dissent and the camp that
would make it obligatory; the one mistakes an antiseptic for a poison,
but the other mistakes it for a diet. Arnold jibed at "the dissidence of
dissent" as an enemy of culture; for us, it becomes an enemy of maturity and wisdom when it is proclaimed as the solitary route to intellectual and moral enlightenment. For it is hardly a route at all; it is
rather a small road-machine that cuts down weeds before they move
in from the shoulders and obstruct the right of way. Some of the
querulous middle-aged seemed bound to delude youth into supposing
that swinging a handsome scythe is finer than, and a substitute for, all
the engineering, surveying, and selection of routes that sometimes lead
to knowledge and wisdom. Or, to drop this highway figure, I have
the feeling that many a lament over supposed lack of spirit was in effect a cry to youth: get out of line, sing off key, be insecure, go on
your nerve—and you will be a man. Here are, at best, a saddening
confusion and a notable irony: for we should have been trying, not to
sell such easy, fruitless programs, but to find appropriate difficulties
that would adequately tap that young energy and lead it toward some
real end. We should have tried to commit them to the one hard exploit
really worthy of a strong and maturing mind—the exacting, taxing,
troubling lifelong enterprise of securing a constantly deepening view of
truth. Instead we harangued them in terms that led both innocent souls
and precious rascals to identify freedom of spirit with letting all whims
fly and egos rip. Instead of encouraging them in the burdensome task

of identifying their own positions and scrutinizing these rigorously, we sold them a complacent and indiscriminate oppositionism, with only the defects of others as targets: for the hard vision of reality they were offered the facile delights of marksmanship. This is less the difficult, not always exciting, pursuit of truth than the glamorous melodrama of one's own sure truth against the certain untruths of others. And how extraordinarily well we succeeded.

If our principles were shaky, I am not sure that the observations on which they were based were any more secure. In my view the students of the fifties were much better students than those of the period since 1967. They were more open to the material, more maturely critical, less doctrinaire, less arrogant. They acted grown-up instead of stridently demanding to be treated as grown-ups. They were more skeptical in the best sense, that is, much less likely to be taken in by the edicts of various secular vaticans. But even if they were, as some still suppose, afflicted with a premature fatigue of mind and soul, they were less suffering from a disease peculiar to the fifties than exemplifying an element which is very deep in our culture—a certain flaccidity of spirit which is summed up in the term "Pushbotton Age." In trying to cure them of that, with which all of us of course are as much afflicted as they, we urged them into another spiritual flaw—the mistaken energizing of perennial attack on the way things are. The great dilemma of American culture is that rather than finding a livable via media it oscillates between two extremes—inactivity and hyperactivity. On the one hand it wants to loaf; on the other it wants to rip things up and make resting impossible for everybody. The rip-things-up temper has been so much in evidence since 1967 that it is tempting to inveigh against it. We may go on into revolution and its horrors and its aftermath, which will only compound the imperfections that provide the nominal target of revolution. But even with that possibility present to the imagination, my own guess is that the lust of loafing is a stronger element in the national personality, and the one from which there is the greater long-range danger. Behind all our deceptive self-congratulation about doing away with brutalizing hardship, with deforming and killing toil, we betray an inner addiction to being comfortable and idle, to giving up work and having a regular life of vacations, to a vacated life in which an atrophying personality finds its natural end in what the ads glorify under different terms—namely, retirement before one has grown up. In the fifties we abused youth for this instead of abusing ourselves, and we offered him a sad way out, summoning him to a heroic hellionism, entrapping him in the romantic melodrama of the querulous outsider, the habitual antagonist, the tormentor of guardians: down with what is up, out with what is in. In
146

this melodrama evil is identified with the haves and ins, and the man on the white charger really finds himself on a merry-go-round horse: riding again the ancient circuit of outsider to ejector to insider to ejectee, or, as it has been otherwise put, from envying to being envied, from blame to guilt. The real problem, that of expanding and improving havehood and inhood, is met no better by the equally deplorable countermelodrama in which youth is urged to glorify his spirit by pouring boiling oil on the spitefully covetous attackers of the citadel held by good insiders. But in regretting a social atmosphere which instead of encouraging maturity through self-understanding preserves immaturity by offering, or seeming to offer, only a choice of melodramatic heroisms, I do not invite youth to blame a prolonged unripeness on parents who have not grown up, and thus to copy their vices, or to revenge himself upon them by casting them into outer darkness. This would be to let him substitute the melodrama of self-defense for the obligation of self-inspection, without which he does not earn defense. I do want to defend him against both a misconceived comfort that implies premature senility, and a misconceived discomfort which would doom him to short pants (or blue jeans) for a lifetime.

As for ourselves we could start by revolting against our own pushbuttonism, which under its old name of sloth used to be considered deadly, and which is symbolized today in the faith that a car without a gearshift represents a superior order of life. The pushbutton mystique is the visionary face of what we have long called scientism, which is not science but the popular religion of science—the faith in a benevolent omnipotence that is, by a series of miracles, irresistibly creating a new paradise now. This doctrine of the millennium-while-you-wait is melodramatic too: friendly magicians either conjure the earth and make riches gush forth, or destroy all our enemies; nowadays, as all newspaper readers know, the word *killer* principally signifies heart ailment or other standard terminal diseases, all beset by clinical St. Georges tracking them to their dragon lairs and doing them in.

Let me break off the familiar story of scientism to recall the melodrama that I left unresolved in the first section of this paper: our professional melodrama of the humanities against the sciences. You will remember that, though a humanist, I found myself unwilling to join in this conflict, just as, though decidedly middle-aged, I wish to absent myself from the melodrama of age against 1950s youth (which had a scarcely happy aftermath). In the former melodrama some humanists made science the villain, and in the latter melodrama we found a wrongdoer who seems at least a cousin of science. Yet science is not the villain; that is too easy a way out.

But before I try to define the actual drama that I believe underlies

147

these dubious melodramas, I want to take another look at the recent American theater. For there we find still another melodrama having a good run.

I refer to the perennial attack, usually mounted by both humanists and scientists, against Education and Educators (both with the capital E). Whether the attack continues in its old role as a kind of sport—say a fox hunt in which a delightful hue and cry in some excited country leaves the general race of foxes living on unharmed and unshaken—or deepens into a systematic extermination really meant to clean up the land, this depends on how we understand the issue. Some of our trouble has been that we have not understood it well, or have not been willing to. Hounding the Educators has been an inspiriting recreation in which we have all had a merry fling; concocting epigrams against colleges of Education has been a delectable form of play, the helplessness of the victims to reply in kind being compensated for by their magnificent self-assurance and singular political cunning. It has been a game of darts with live but pain-free targets, a show in which highbrows could for once enjoy the lowlife of audience participation, a melodrama in which eggheads could virtuously throw dead eggs at living villains. Now there is the genesis of the trouble: the shrinking of life into a melodrama with villains—viewing Educators as racketeers plotting against an innocent society, breaching the life of us good people with a barrage of evil ideas.

The truth is that Educators do not have bad ideas; indeed they do not really *have* ideas at all. They are a channel for ideas of ours, often hidden ideas, which they carry into the flexible scholastic forms. We must see that they are no more than the agents of a view of life to which our culture is deeply committed and that we cannot wipe out the agents without cleaning up the view of life. We believe in the preeminence of technique or what we fondly call "know-how" (one could base a modern cultural history on the decline of *savoir faire* into know-how), and we can hardly be surprised if education falls into the hands of entrepreneurs who claim to have cornered the market of educational techniques. We have no answer for them. Enthralled by the mystique of technique, we invent gorgeous verbal robes that, however suitable for reverent worship, keep us from seeing things in sharp outline; even Ph.D.'s in the humanities talk with sonorous awe of their "methodologies," when all they mean is their methods, which are quite a different thing. Where, then, do we find the lucidity needed to see through the methodistic religion? We can hardly demand that technique yield to substance, for our ideas of substance have been badly eroded by our skeptical attitudes. If we complain about ineffec-

148

tive teaching of reading, writing, and arithmetic, we engage in some self-deception; for one thing, we hardly provide the examples of devoted reading which might make young observers regard reading as a built-in human activity; more fundamentally, we pay mostly lip service to these skills, which at heart we regard as mainly ornamental and by no means requisite to that getting along in, or reforming of, the world that we really believe in. If we find the public schools becoming trade schools, it is because trades are our real article of faith. If we find schools teaching adjustment rather than training minds, it is because with a sharp diagnostic eye the schoolmen have spotted a couple of faiths that, whatever we profess, we really act upon. The first of these is that getting along in the group is invariably better than developing one's own genius. I will call this communitarianism, and by communitarianism I mean a perversion of the true sense of community, with which even eccentricity is compatible, into a constant organizing or rather managing of all life by group activities that eliminate privacy and what it contributes to maturity—group sings, sports, projects, club and lodge rule, and, above all, a glorifying and universalizing of committees that tends to starve out all realms of activity not amenable to committeefication. Communitarianism means the joining principle: once a joiner was a skilled craftsman, but now he is a crafty politician or a man afraid of himself. The other faith of ours that the schools have caught hold of and modeled themselves upon is that what is called "personality" is the center of all human values. If, then, the schools do little for minds, it is either that mind is unimportant to us or that, with its suggestion of individual talent, *mind* is almost a naughty four-letter word. Sometimes we sneak in mind-value under the name of *brains*, but by it we tend to mean caginess in worldly operations. Our real passion is for "personality," a sort of mass-pleasing demeanor that can be boned up even by, or perhaps best by, the untalented. This is the opposite of the thoughtful and the reflective; hence in 95 percent of American facial photography, the obscene display of teeth, the oral cheesecake (to which the grim humorless faces of the latter 1960s were a sorry antidote). In part, of course, such attitudes are a bastard offspring of democracy, in which the majority principle, when it is given an unqualified universal application, can lead to the exaltation of mediocrity and a preoccupation with mean ends.

So we cannot rest content with a melodramatic attack on Educational villains as if they were simply plotting against a highminded citizenry. If we really want to do away with the present breed of them, we have to expect not only to hurt but also to be hurt. A large job of extermination means at least a little bit of suicide. Fortunately this is one suicide that can be followed by a rebirth.

149

Now, at last, what are the common plot elements in these diverse popular melodramas? On one stage we saw the humanists wanting to cut down the scientists; on another the fifties youth being harassed for not being, like the young lady in *Oklahoma!*, wild and free (and rebounding into an extraordinarily wild and free melodrama of their own); on another, habitual hissing at Educational villains for taking us where they saw, and we didn't know, we wanted to go.

A key complaint against Education is perhaps our key. I mean the complaint that the schools spend too much time on fringe subjects and fail to teach the solid science that can produce good modern physicists. Various reasons for the state of affairs have been advanced, but there is one which, if it has been mentioned at all, has apparently received little attention: I mean the simple fact that fringes are more *easy* than central subjects. If science is badly taught, it is because it is easier that way, and if potential good physicists are not coming out of high schools, it is because the study of physics is not easy. For it takes more than adolescent vitality to resist the glorification of ease that implicitly penetrates the whole of our culture. Publicly we talk and reason a comfortiori. A good deal of method-worship is ease-worship. Half our advertising is on the theme of labor-saving and shortcuts; no more backbending, walking, or standing; no more moving really, with power brakes and power steering; learn while you sleep; three easy steps; six easy lessons; utter comfort, still more comfort, colossal comfort; lift the lever, push the button; automatic, automatic, automatic. And if such terms seem to be the characteristic style of gown against town, the fact is that gown has its own forms of sloth. Here I allude not to individual failures of conscience, which are more frequent than they ought to be, but to institutional lapses. The accusation of a tired love of ease which has been leveled at fifties students might more fittingly be leveled at many students of the 1968–72 period. The "pass/ fail" system, as we pretty well know by now, is a lazy man's device; people using the system characteristically do no more than get by. Another form of slothfulness is the distaste for penalties; the "credit/no credit" system wipes out the costs of failure which belong to the reality of life. Both systems conceal the subtle creeping sloth of egalitarianism: the passion of the nonlaboring to deprive those who labor of the fruits of their labor. For the faculty it is easier to fall in with these devices than to resist, and to fall in with the ultimate spirit of the devices by so applying "pass/fail" that it becomes ironically known as "pass/ pass." When such stuff, on both town side and gown side, keeps mushrooming into the air, there is bound to be a fallout with moral consequences: the weakening from generation to generation of the capacity for difficulty and labor which are an eternal part of our destiny. It is

150

the spirit of pushbuttonism which is latent in all these melodramas. Town and gown both reveal it; elders defensively accuse the youth of it; humanists try to pin it on scientists—and then call loudly, in come-one-come-all tones, that they are peddling something good for what ails the mechanized country. In the pushbutton spirit, everyone has a gimmick—that is, a shortcut to salvation. With one fraction of our cultural psyche we invent the gimmick of automatism, with another fraction the gimmick of dissentism and oppositionism, and with another, alas, the gimmick of humanism.

In the early 1970s the situation is not very encouraging, for fewer people are studying science; they don't like the hard work. If they don't like hard work, either they will learn nothing from the humanities, or the humanities will destroy themselves by catering to people who prefer rap sessions and gut reactions to discipline. We see now the way in which the sciences and the humanities have more to bring them together than to separate them. For the problem is less to prevent the subsumption of all reality under physical law (a confusion most likely to be fostered by science-bewitched humanists), less to uphold the historical, aesthetic, intuitive, and contemplative visions of reality (which often the scientists are the first to defend), than it is to maintain the two great areas of thought, with their complementary formulations and insights and wrestlings with truth, against the religion of techniques, the religion of ease, the naive faith in panaceas, and the secret lust for mediocrity that is the final enemy of the great mind and the great imagination.

We can restate all this by saying that our problem is the problem of excellence and of our particular ways of fleeing from it to cheaper mistresses. To be for excellence, I suppose, is rather like being against sin; it may seem only to betray one's cynicism, one's naiveté, or one's passion for what can be taken for granted. I wish I could believe that we do take the pursuit of excellence for granted. But this is not the evidence of our schools, which institutionalize the half-articulate leanings of the community—the identification of achievement with what many can do or want to do; and the decay of the concept of wise leisure, the only rationale of a mechanized age, into a sense that toil is evil in itself and that the quality of life is a function of magical electronics and of passive reception of not only luxuries but necessities, tendered with expert slavery by a finally defeated nature (the ultimate permanent colony of a universal imperialism).

The danger of sciences and humanities to each other is infinitesimal compared with the danger to both from a decay of the feeling for excellence that both have to stand on. That decay occurs when the moral energies required by the pursuit of excellence are drained off into a melodramatic factionalism. We could as well say fractionalism, for melodrama is the world of fractions, where part-truths are mistaken for wholes, and where half-truth disease is countered by half-truth remedies. We have noted the terms that chart the reduction of valid concepts, in which the ideal of excellence is inherent, into fractional ideas that are the more harmful because they resemble the original wholes. We have long been familiar with scientism, which is an amputated version of the pursuit of physical knowledge—namely, the popular faith in the effortless life of secular miracles: a faith which scientists themselves recoil from because for love of truth it substitutes a lust for utilities. Learning from science the importance of techniques and methods, we have fallen into a fanatic methodism that leaves us helpless among technophile schoolmen because they and we alike beg the question of what it is that is to be delivered through their mysterious know-how. If we do think of the what, we also suffer from the shrinkage of concepts. The democracy which is an enemy of false distinctions slides into a democratism which threatens all distinction, and the need of community into a clattery, busybody communitarianism. This semitruth in turn begets the semitruth dissentism, the hardening and narrowing—the arteriosclerosis, really—of the respect for, and tolerance of, spontaneous dissent; dissentism is the inculcation or practice of a habitual contrariety that mistakes, for the achievement of truth, what is at best, for some people, a preliminary to the search for truth, and that reduces to a sort of lark, a lively picnickers' flight from stodginess, the sober, agonizing earning of freedom that requires more years than most of us will give to it.

Now back to the beginning and to the initial undefined term, the undiagnosed ailment—to what we called humanisticism. By now the sense of it should be clear. It is the humanities' contribution to the fraternity of mutations in which appear scientism, methodism, democratism, communitarianism, and dissentism. *Humanisticism* sounds awkward and swollen; it has the dropsy of syllables that often afflicts sociology. So much the better to describe the flawed humanism which becomes a gimmick, a shortcut, a panacea, an easy-to-take tonic. So much the better to describe what happens when a decent humanism becomes a competitor in the market, gets organized in a protective and promotional way, and slips into a sort of ecclesiastical business, intent on swelling its congregation, enlarging its acreage, and expanding its soteriological claims. It is humanisticism which mistakes the educational symptom for the cultural illness, confuses quarrelsomeness with the free spirit, and does not distinguish scientism, the enemy of humanism, from science, its fellow. In such ways is humanisticism, the melodramatic factionalism of the humanities, deflected from the proper course of excellence.

The men of letters whom I have so far happened to quote are all, I

suddenly realize, Victorians. If differences among them let me survive
even a casual reliance upon ancestors of diminished repute, I can perhaps take a final risk and invoke a classicist, in fact, invoke an ancient
one through a modern one. While writing these pages I could not put
out of my memory a passage in Horace's "Poetics" that had vaguely
suggested itself as relevant, that passage in which Horace claims that in
other affairs mediocrity is admissible sometimes, but in poetry never.
The most pungent translation is Ben Jonson's: "But neither men, nor
gods, nor bookstores meant,/ Poets should ever be indifferent." If any
serious poem, Horace goes on, falls short of the summit, it plunges
toward the depths. Or in Jonson's slightly amplified version:

> So any poem, fancied, or forth-brought
> To bett'ring of the mind of man, in aught,
> If ne'er so little it depart the first,
> And highest, sinketh to the lowest and worst.

Or as it is bluntly put by a quite different character, our contemporary
Felix Krull, Thomas Mann's picaro who is really an artist, "a performance had to be masterly if it was not to be ridiculous." The poetry
that is Horace's subject, and the dramatic art that is Mann's, are central
enough to stand symbolically for the humanities in general; so that the
categorical demand of excellence in poem or performance not only
applies to all the works of mind and imagination that are the primary
humanities, but can be extended as well into the working principles
and actual working of us secondary humanists. Here I have been looking at only one of our problems, trying to say that excellence is not
served by seeing all defects and ills and dangers in terms of ne'er-do-
wells, scapegoats, and ill-favored rascals that we can polish off or cut
down to size as if we were heroes of melodrama. This is too easy, and
it smells of the gimmick. Excellence and ease are not compatible; we
literary humanists do not suppose them to be so in our professional
work, so that we need hardly combine them as we meditate a role in
an imperfect culture. I will leave it to others' imagination to discover
the social equivalent of the difficult task of scholarship, the taxing critical analysis, the exhausting creation of a drama, none of which has a
single easy target. But if the artist, to take one example only, does
shrink from the excellence that demands too much of him and settles
for writing a melodrama, we ask at least that he know what he is doing. So if we do ever fall into melodramatic courses in troubled times,
we should at least not delude ourselves about what we do. If we can,
remember the hard drama for which the melodrama is a substitute.

14
Humanistic Education as Comedy

A Funambulist's Analogy

In "Humanisticism and Melodrama" I talked about the ways in which the humanities, by insisting on how good they are, can manage not to look as good as they are. Now I propose a more difficult theme—the ways in which the humanities can both look good and be good by doing the difficult thing they have to do. In the preceding essay I talked about the kinds of melodrama that we humanists (not to mention some others) drift into. Now I will talk about the kinds of melodrama that interested parties want to force us into. At the same time, as my title makes clear, I am going to make a central shift from melodrama to another genre, comedy. But I am temporarily postponing definition and explanation. I will play for a final faint touch of mystery.

So I start with a quotation from one of the very bright, at times dazzling, literary lights of our day, Anthony Burgess. In a rather off-the-cuff style several years ago, Burgess was naming some of the ingredients of comedy. Two of these are close to the heart of the matter: as Burgess puts it, "acceptance of the world" and "[acceptance] of the fundamental disparateness of all the elements of the world." There are other ways of defining comedy, but Burgess's works well. It is compact, current, consistent with comic practice, and faintly cryptic. The key words are "acceptance" and "world." A curious view? Well, to get a feeling for what goes on in comedy, let us see what other options we have when we have to decide what to do about the world. We can distinguish, on the one hand, between "acceptance of the world," and, on the other, "mastery" of the world, "transformation" of the world, "rejection" of the world, "withdrawal" from the world, "punishment" of the world, and, in the opposite direction, "submission" to the world. We will differentiate later between "accept" and

154

"submit." For the moment, we need only see that the choices are numerous. They are made more numerous, and certainly more subtle, when we take into account Burgess's second phrase, "acceptance of disparateness." In time we will work disparateness into the picture.

At this point I break off to propose my funambulist's analogy, though it may seem lightminded or downright wrongheaded. I suggest that in humanistic education we are engaged in an enterprise whose dimensions are comic. I hasten to come on with a shot of verbal tranquilizer: I do not mean silly or trifling, that is, unserious. Oh no, serious enough, especially in a world that rivals the Victorians when it comes to the importance of being earnest. I mean rather that the relations of us schoolmen are with the world, properly understood, and that our basic mode is one of acceptance, properly understood. This perhaps murky metaphor is meant only as a touch of dramatic foreshadowing. It is not a reveille by outrage, that scandalizing of readers by which a critic sometimes assures himself that he is an intellectual alarm clock breaking at last the long sleep of the torpid multitude.

I have now tipped my hand and shown that I want to approach humanistic education through a recent preoccupation of mine—the exploring of genres and the endeavor, however halting, to frame some generic theory. This procedure may seem to border on contempt of court by violating the frequent decree that art and life must be kept apart. Nevertheless parallels between some aspects of art and some aspects of life are illuminating, and in the end, I suspect, these are rooted in identical or comparable functions of the human psyche. Because as human beings we are as we are, we invoke similar energies and moods in aesthetic and in day-to-day relationships. We act in somewhat the same ways when we create or experience high comedy, and when we pursue humanistic education. I will proceed somewhat indirectly toward the logic at the heart of this analogy that may now seem eccentric.

Suppose we think of a genre as a very specific mode of relationship between the individual and experience, between the human personality and the larger arena of action, be it social or political or cosmic. Genres persist because they organize and interpret experience in constant ways that we find persuasive. Farce, for instance, presents experience as temporarily confused, frustrating, and irrational, but as finally innocuous and as resuming familiar order. Naturalistic drama interprets life as indifferent or hostile and ultimately disastrous. Farce exists, so to speak, because we long for, and occasionally need, freedom from rational reliability, emotional and physical vulnerability, and moral accountability. In farce we do not reason or behave as we should, and

155

yet the retribution is nominal or ceremonial; we insult and knock down others, but we neither hurt them nor face more than formalistic revenge; we are insulted and knocked down, but we do not really hurt. Instead of the blows of fate we feel only the mild cushiony bounce of the inflated bladder; we are not stung by the moral birch-rod but brushed by the mock-moral slapstick. At the other end of the spectrum tragedy exists because we are capable of feeling a profound conflict of loyalties, or because we are capable of feeling, at the same time, both a sweeping passion and the imperative that tries to contain the passion. In farce we have all the privileges of insentience; in tragedy we are wholly sentient, to both good and evil. In farce we relish being partially human or nonhuman; in tragedy we have to experience our fullest humanity. In both, the form responds to a human need or capacity—a need for vacation from, or a capacity for a total range of, moral experience. Generic forms derive from different longings and capabilities, from an unconscious questing for adequately various kinds of psychic exercise.

Under the pressure, then, of what we want and need to do and feel, and of what we can and must do and feel, we respond to the world in different basic ways. Each response has two aspects: it emerges from a facet of human personality, and it achieves formal expression in a stable generic style. Instead of accepting the world, one may struggle to master it, and one may succeed or succumb. Either way the generic style is that of melodrama, be it melodrama of triumph or melodrama of defeat. On the one hand we have Marlowe's Tamburlaine, and on the other, though with a host of complications, Shakespeare's Richard III. One of the complications is that in Richard III there is, along with the conqueror who fails, something of the con man. The con man's conquest is of a hit-and-run type, a tour de force, a victory of wit against the odds; through him we let fly with our latent rascally inclinations to put one over on the world. This is the picaresque mode—still melodrama, but with the conqueror turned trickster. In this mode, I surmise, we create and delight in Jonson's Volpone; when a rogue operates against a world of rogues, we join with the bolder roguery of an urban Tamburlaine.

Withdrawing from the world is a different kettle of tea; we leave the tea table, where we encounter others and make drama, and take to solitary sipping. Here we practice the lyric mode, perhaps indeed to comment on the world, as Wordsworth did, but characteristically to explore the reality within (we of course want the world's ear to vindicate the personal voice). At times we want to withdraw from, at other times to reject, the world; the modes I take to be different, look alike though they may. Withdrawal is an affirmative choice of a differ-

156

ent scene of reality—be it the inner scene, or, as it may appear to the chooser, a transcendental scene manifested only to the unique man's inner eye. Rejection, however, is pure negation. In Wordsworth's *The Borderers* the satanic Oswald argues to the outsider Marmaduke that crime is at once the best route to freedom and the best critique of society—a singularly modern view. This pathological rejection of the world may be balanced against a more rational rejection of it in Molière's *Misanthrope*: Alceste banishes society from his life because of what he has learned about himself. But he does this only after he has mercilessly scarified society. He has exemplified the principal mode of rejection, satire. Satire is the scourging kind of melodrama: it contains the traditional conflict of good man as satirist versus the bad men of the world. The dramatist may be the good man himself, or he may have his agents in the play, or he may scourge evil by showing its impact on its victims. Pinter takes this last tack in *The Birthday Party*, in which he very freshly presents the satirized social order through two sinister characters who seem more like gunmen or racketeers than insider-oppressors.

The most rigorous way of rejecting the world is to punish it. The dramatist may do this through his sympathy with the denunciatory voice in his drama, e.g., that of Manly in Wycherley's *Plain Dealer* or of Bosola in *The Duchess of Malfi*. Or he may portray the punitive spirit in action, and thus write revenge melodrama. Timon of Athens engages in wholesale verbal revenge against a world made ignoble, it seems to him, by ingratitude. The Duchess of Malfi's brothers show the punitive spirit in almost pure form. In Duerrenmatt's *The Visit* Claire Zachanassian retaliates fiercely against both the individual who was false to her long ago and the community that drove her out. Now, wealthy, she pays an enormous sum to the town to murder her original seducer, and she thus effects the subtlest double revenge in drama: the unjust man loses his life, and the town that kills him for money loses its soul. Yet there is a still subtler kind of revenge melodrama: in it, the revenger's malice precedes any act that can incite revengefulness. (It may even provoke the actions that will then make retaliation seem equitable.) In *The Revenger's Tragedy* Tourneur all but discovers an aptness for revenge as a radical element in personality; Vendice, the title character, does have grounds for revenge, but one feels that if they hadn't come up, Vendice would have instigated them. The need for revenge that precedes the cause appears more subtly in Iago. It is only a short leap from Vendice and Iago to the arsonists in Max Frisch's *Firebugs*: they are Iago in modern dress. We often hear, now, that poverty breeds crime, a gesture of revenge against society. But long before this sense of cause became possible for us, Shakespeare saw

157

that moral poverty breeds revengefulness. If one is underprivileged in spirit—in capacity to love others or accept the world—one cannot bear the existence of those who come closer to affluence of heart. Dollar-poverty is remediable; soul-poverty is not. Everywhere it will find —in the very existence of anyone who has a share of evident well-being—slights and affronts that cry for revenge. Frisch has caught the very core of this in Schmitz and Eisenring, whose destruction of the world is the ultimate revenge upon it and punishment of it.

I have saved until last two ways of responding to the world that are in contrast not only with each other but with the acceptance that Burgess attributes to comedy—namely, transformation of the world and submission to it. One belongs to the utopian, the other to the cynic; the dramatist may be either one himself, or portray either one. Transformationist drama and collusionist drama exist widely at popular levels which are not our business: all kinds of reform plays and all kinds of success plays; throw-the-rascals-out plots and local-boy-makes-good plots. It is one step up from popular drama to Ibsen's *An Enemy of the People,* a reform drama that nevertheless takes on an interesting ambiguity: the would-be transformer of the world has an admirable integrity, but also a frantic romantic self-acceptance that makes him a little ridiculous. The more memorable transformationist dramas verge on the tragic: a certain intransigence of things as they are, or of people as they are, reveals the hopeful transformer as foolishly utopian or essentially hubristic. The title character in Brecht's *St. Joan of the Stockyards* would help sweep away the old evil but by a sort of original fallibility falls short in her mission. Like reformers, reformees may not be up to utopia. Ibsen's *Wild Duck* presents archetypally the ruin of reformees when their low-key adjustment to actuality is undermined by a remorseless pusher of the ideal; even the latter then edges toward the tragic consciousness.

Then there are three more recent plays in which kings or strong men attempt to transform the world by fiat. Two of these are by Duerrenmatt, *The Marriage of Mr. Mississippi* and *An Angel Comes to Babylon.* In the former, a Puritan and a Marxist want to force their brands of salvation upon the world; in the latter, King Nebuchadnezzar declares a New Order which obliquely reflects various modern reformist programs. Ironically both worlds resist instant millennialization; and still more ironically the would-be transformers of the world turn out to be less moved by a workable ideal than, as so often in life, by their egos, their love of power, and even their revengefulness. But they never come quite into the self-awareness that would shift the play from the realm of rather complex melodrama into that of tragedy. That shift into tragedy is more nearly made in Dorothy

158

Sayers's *The Devil to Pay,* in which the hero is an up-to-date Doctor Faustus. This modern power-plunger—I quote Miss Sayers's own words—is "the impulsive reformer, over-sensitive to suffering, impatient of the facts, eager to set the world right by a sudden overthrow, in his own strength and regardless of the ineluctable nature of things." It is a fascinating interpretation of the Faustian passion to transcend all limits.

If the transformation of society ordinarily leads, as these examples suggest, to different kinds of melodrama and at times to the edge of tragedy, there is one great drama in which the remaking of the world ends in a general social happiness that is one index of the comic mode. This is of course Aristophanes' *Lysistrata,* which, with our present coloring of consciousness, we might call not only the first antiwar play but also the first woman's lib drama. Women take over an irrational world of war that men have made and cure it: they do away with war by applying to sex the method that America would later apply to drink—prohibition and timely repeal. It is a jeu d'esprit that in our own day might be done by Ionesco: the practical joke as morality play. And when I say practical joke, I reveal the enormous irony here: the transformation of the world, which is not the material of comedy, is brought about largely by the basic formula of farce, that is, the sense of people as mechanisms or robots who can respond only in a certain way. Press the right buttons—or in this case keep them from being pressed—and the machine which looks like a man will do and say what it should. There are no human complexities to color, distort, or mar the desired response. Sex-starve man, and you will quickly demilitarize him.

Let us shift to the opposite attitude to the world. Here we do not alter the world but fall in with it—submit to it, cooperate with it as we sometimes say euphemistically, or practice collusion with it. We do what we have to do to get on, to get in, to make out, to go up, to beat the game, to save our skins, to come out on top, to prevent going under, dropping out, getting axed, losing our shirts, taking the rap. We learn the score, the rules, the price, the odds, the percentages, bargains, trade-ins; we learn about fall guys, con men, city hall, people who have something, people who have something on us, people who know something; about clay feet, Achilles heels, the well-heeled, soft touches, hard heads, thick skins, thin stories. I am of course describing the kinds of response that create black comedy. Black comedy is in one way akin to farce: in it we are functioning with a diminishment of humanity. Our emotional and moral responsiveness has a subnormal temperature. But, in contrast with farce, our minds act vigorously in one area—not the reflective or evaluative, but the operational. How do we, in the world, put one over, make a deal, work something out, hang on? We plan, arrange, calculate; we live with it, we take what we have to, but we do not get sick, hurt, bleed, or cry out. We refrain from these plaints of wounded humanity, not because we are heroic or stoic, but because in this mode we have by definition excluded the expectable sensitivity that would generate tears, shock, moans, and screams. In black comedy everyone is adjusted, but because of the ways in which we need to think about ourselves, we feel that the accepted adjustment would, for us, leave too much out. Hence we use the adjective "black." In Machiavelli's *Mandragola* everybody from priest to husband and wife to wife's mother is made happy by an arrangement whereby the foolish husband provides access to his wife for the man who wants to be, and thus becomes, her lover. The play is sometimes called a satire, but it is hard to see it as such, for it includes no dramatic assertion of an alternative standard which would invite criticism of the mode of life depicted. To jump ahead to the nineteenth century, Henry Becque's *Parisian Woman* shows a cool woman, with great wit and ingenuity, conning a husband and two different lovers, so that each of the three is convinced that it is he alone who has the key to her heart, and to her quarters. (Becque's plays of this kind were known as "comédies rosses," that is, "beastly" or "nasty" comedies—an interesting alternative metaphor for the type.) Then in our own day we find the black mode almost classically figured forth in Joe Orton's *Entertaining Mr. Sloane*. In this play the protagonist renders himself vulnerable by various indiscretions, including murder. Consequently when two people have the goods on him and apply a little twist of blackmail, he finds paying the price the better part of valor. The two who have the goods on him are a sister and brother, she nymphomaniac, he homosexual; and to both of them the man who can't resist them is an irresistible sexual plum. So, with neo-Solomonic shrewdness, they divide him between them: he will spend six months with one, and six with the other. In the hero's submission to what has to be we see the spirit of black comedy: playing ball with the world in its lowest common denominator. It is significant that the three plays in which Shakespeare explores the themes of playing ball with the world have been called "dark" comedies: the term itself suggests how far along the road to black comedy Shakespeare goes.

I have been speaking of literary forms, mainly dramatic ones, as embodying our different basic modes of relationship with the world. We find similar formulations of experience on the stage and in the literal life lived outside the theater. Both of these can be referred to fundamental habits of the mind, or even structures of the mind, which lead us into persistent styles of response. So we are talking about basic patterns of action that manifest themselves triply—in the human personality, in the theater, and in society.

The human dividedness which is the source of tragic form can appear in rending conflicts of loyalty in daily life. We dread dividedness, and we are addicted to various simplistic moldings of reality where we can be at one with ourselves. There is a latent conqueror in all of us; he takes over the personalities of enough individuals to create many rulers in the world—once military, now mostly political and financial, wielding power by office or charisma. Hence the melodrama of triumph. But we also feel guilty about conquest, we feel envious, we sense inequity between talents and dreams; so we cherish the theme of how-are-the-mighty-fallen, from politicians to athletes (this mood once created a subgenre, loosely called "*de casibus* tragedy"). We dwell on the theme that power corrupts, especially others; we cut them down, and we approve the fates of Macbeths, Faustuses, and Julius Caesars. In this, another subtle impulse, probably unrecognized, gets into play: to avoid fashionable terms let us call it the impulse to go down, give up, or fade out, because outer forces are large, and we are small. Dropouts were a human phenomenon long before our day; people have always resigned or become resigned; felt hopelessly pressed, oppressed, depressed. Hence that strange sense of kinship with Richard II, or with Synge's riders to the sea, or even with such disintegrating people as those in Gorki's *Lower Depths* or O'Neill's *Iceman*. On the other hand, in all of us there is a rascal or a would-be rascal; some of us do become con men or sneakingly envy successful rogues; or we can exercise these normally concealed proclivities by creating or relishing the picaresque side of Richard III or Volpone or Mosca or Frank Wedekind's Marquis of Keith. Few of us do not have some share of the impulse to pull back or pull out or step down and make do in a private or nonrelational domain. We don't surrender, but withdraw; we find hermitages, nunneries male or female, ivory towers, or play pens; we retire early, plan rural hideaways, or take sanctuary in pubs or Pacific paradises. We can understand as well as practice the lyric role, be it erotic, threnodic, or meditative; we can slily extend its power by declaring that my mind to me a kingdom is. Since academic halls are sometimes called ivory towers, we might think of our style as lyric rather than comic, with mental kingdoms full of the tunes of professorial power. But few of us sing, or want to sing, in private; we want whole opera houses full of ears to be enchanted by our notes. Our symbol is the PA system rather than an intercom system within the kingdom of the mind; our ivory tower somehow acquires broadcast antennae.

161

To return from academic man to secular everyman: we are all re-markably equipped for that kind of melodrama in which we reject the world, that is, resent it, pan it, flog it, and enjoy fantasies of revenge upon it. With our sensitive egos we often think of it as unworthy of us, ungrateful, crass, indecent, and hostile. We editorialize against it, complain about it, vote it down. With this sense of rectitude and de-serts within, and frailty and inequity all about, we become satirists and find in satirical art a catharsis for our distress. When the distress be-comes pathological, or when inner disorder creates a sense of unbear-able wrongness in the world, we set out to destroy it, by philosophical diatribe or by bombs. In this sickness, surely, a few let grow madly a destructiveness of which the seeds are in all of us. Oddly, annihilation-ism can rarely go with its own feet or face: the black sheep of malice nearly always makes like the white horse of salvation. Most of us also have our own stables of authentic white horses; we ride abroad car-rying the light by which the world may be transformed. We conde-scend to ourselves as we once were, and invent ideas of progress, uto-pian schemes, millennial visions. Nowadays recipes, movements, cru-sades are everywhere; assorted secular missionaries assert that the kingdom of god is at hand, or urge us to midwifery in its behalf. But, opposite the transformationists, the children of the world keep shrewdly observing how things go, where things lead, and what things to do. Some hate the rules, some want to change them, some to do away with them; others find out what they let you get away with.

Because we are what we are, in thought and feeling, we make far-ces, melodramas, satires, picaresque works, tragedies, even nihilistic works, and we adopt comparable styles in our relationships with oth-ers and with society. Hence we are talking about a trinity of interre-lated theaters: the inner theater of our own nature, the theater where plays are enacted, and then, all the world, which, as we know only too well, is a stage.

Next point then: where does humanistic education fit into this theat-rical scheme? First we can guess or assume that education is not certain things. We have to hope that it isn't farce, though now and then we fall on our faces. At times, indeed, we may seem to have that blessed freedom from decent emotion, expected moral awareness, and average capacity for thought that is the comfort of the farcical world, but this is an aberration. Faculty as well as students are prone to emotion and injury, particularly hurt feelings; and our hurt feelings tend to trans-pose themselves into moral indignation—all this quite nonfarcical. Granted, we use a lot of machinery; repetition is inevitable; and we deal with relatively large numbers. Hence we do hear charges of mechanization—charges, that is, of living in a farce, with high-speed ups and downs, ins and outs, round and rounds. The charge serves my purpose, for it represents the accurate view that we should be doing something other than farce. On the other hand, education is not a tragic process, in which a good man comes to wisdom after catastrophes, for himself and others, that arise out of his own divided nature. Of course there is always some dividedness in institutions and their inmates, but it is rarely catastrophic; there are always some disasters, but they are rarely central and representative; we traffic more in knowledge than in wisdom, and suffering and agonized self-confrontation are rare. Granted, in the last year or two some of us have shown a certain facility in what I will call *mea-culpa-tion*, that is, declaring rather loudly that we have done wrong and had better do better. This sounds like tragic self-recognition, but I fear it is pseudotragic. It means panic rather than true anagnorisis, and the *mea* in *mea culpa* tends to mean *tua*. When we sound like tragic Lear, "I have done her wrong," we are pretty likely to be hinting at some other educator's vice.

That is, we drift easily into melodrama, innocence lined up against guilt. Town accuses gown, and we cry out, "Who? Me?" We have not loafed at the lectern, lusted only for the library, or feasted at sabbatical fleshpots. From exculpation we turn to accusation of our own; we scream back at town, "anti-intellectualism." We all tend to be good guys and get the drop on bad guys. But despite such melodramatic gestures, basic educational patterns are not melodramatic. War and politics are society's melodrama, and in academe we are not really in a battle, whatever day-to-day engagements may crop up. We are not engaged in conquest or triumph. If we drift into an image of ourselves as white knights of light beheading the dirty dragon of ignorance, we better watch ourselves, for we should know by now that at best we break even with a love of ignorance that in our day thinks gut reactions are the best way of dealing with food for thought. On the other hand, we hardly feel defeated: in every nighttime of budgets or public disesteem, we feel sure that the humanities have not set for good but will rise again, or shine once more after a short eclipse by the periodic moon of errant human passions.

Finally there are two other modes that we are not—lyric and picaresque. Lyric, as I have said, is too private for us, though we may want to sing with the unfettered personal voice of the lyricist. We do have one touch of the lyric mode, perhaps: the richly tuneful life of the think-tank, whence the free soul releases the inner mind-song to whoever wants to tune in. Clearly education is not picaresque, though it may harbor quite a few rogues. It holds a steady course rather than plays hit and run, its cunning is that of the explicator rather than that of the con man, in values its aim is the long investment rather than the quick profit, and it does not so much live by its wits as sharpen its wits on life.

If I am right, then, we in education are not withdrawing from the world, conquering it, being conquered by it, ridiculing it, punishing it, or tricking it. We now have left three ways of meeting the world—transforming it, accepting it, or yielding to its will. Let us postpone, for the moment, the two extreme styles of response, that is, kicking the world in the pants and playing footsie with the world, and bring them in later and illustratively. We are down, then, to the ways in which our humanistic enterprise embodies the spirit of comedy.

Burgess, to repeat, sees as the primary mark of comedy the acceptance of the world. This may cause an initial shudder in academe, which is somewhat given to viewing the world superciliously. But the shudder comes out of romantic thoughtlessness. The world is a congeries of facts, and a sense of brute facts is the indispensable cornerstone of education, no less in the humanities than elsewhere. We cannot ignore—and at times indeed seem wholly content with—the biographic fact, the historical fact, the textual fact, the lexicographic fact, and so on. In another sense, accepting the world is very much like acknowledging one's parents. True, at times we want to be a playboy of the western world and kill our da'. But we can't, really, for such homicide is also suicide. The world supports us, and we will never become self-supporting or inherit the old man's estate. Accepting the world means accepting this fact, and accepting the fact that up to a point the world wants us to support it—in the main, to contribute to its security and sense of continuity. The role is not an unnatural one for the humanities, which can exist only through a sense of essential human continuity, as given form by a stable human imagination, beneath the variant styles of succeeding generations. Naturally we do not promise that all will be the same; we simply use as our implicit base the constants that will cohabit with change.

But when I said that the world wants us to support it, my key phrase was "up to a point." For the world whose creature we are, and which we must accept, really does not call for support all the time. Part of the time, true, it wants us to train the young to carry on; but for at least as much time it cries out, "What must I do to be saved?" Thus the world puts us on a very hot spot, for as a profession we do not know, and cannot know, any specific routes to salvation. I exclude, of course, the occasional real prophet who turns up in this profession, as in other professions, and the more numerous individuals,

164

stout of voice and assured in doctrine, who speak as with prophetic
power, and seek political power with which to engrave their prophe-
cies upon the body of the world.

From the point that the world both bids and asks it is a logical jump
back to the second element in Burgess's definition of comedy, namely,
that comedy accepts "the fundamental disparateness of all the elements
of the world." Literary or theatrical comedy, that is, makes do with
all manner of men, laughing at many, of course, but not treating them
punitively or destructively; it takes in its stride a good deal of self-
seeking, self-deception, calculation, naiveté, and naughtinesses of various kinds—the habits of ordinary sensual men; in a way, all men survive, getting in the main what is due them, little or much. In Congreve's *Way of the World* even the underbred and the overrefined have
their place and are not cast into outer darkness. In Wilder's *Skin of Our
Teeth* we see a range of follies and even of vices, but without indignation or bad temper. In Noël Coward's *Hay Fever,* which I find myself thinking less frothy than I once did, the squares and the artists,
each boring or terrifying the other, make do in their own ways.

The comedy-like world of humanistic education needs to know its
mode of acceptance of disparateness. We can define this in different
ways. One way is to say that we accept both the is and the ought to be
or could be. We belong to an existent world which we cannot simply
deny or reject; the actuality comes out of a human nature which is a
fact of life. But we can also remind it of other facts of life, other human
possibilities, which make alterations possible. In the humanities there
are at least two characteristic ways of accepting disparateness. The
central disparateness is that of human nature itself, and if knowing
that is not what centrally occupies us in the humanities, then I do not
know what does. Everyman is both saint and devil; true, in this man
or at this time, one may speak louder than the other; but we dare not
forget that both are there. In cynical moods we forget the saint; in
utopian moods, the devil. We can translate our sense of disparateness
into other idioms: we accept the romantic and the realistic in man, the
rational and the irrational, the necessity of work as well as of leisure;
we know that he needs freedom but likewise deeply craves bounds
and bonds, that he seeks the required as well as the chosen. And we
better know that he is both conservative and liberal, that being both is
indispensable, and that both contain the seeds of both vice and virtue.
This duality of awareness is a central business of the humanities, and
without it our educational procedures will go haywire.

Put it in another perspective, even a risky one: we accept disparateness when we are open both to the traditional and the new, the supra-
historical and the topical, the timeless and the timely. I call this risky

because in our day there is so heavy a putsch for academic emphasis on immediate ends that the humanist strategy of balance would compel us to insist on the nontemporal identities of life, whether or not they appear to serve the new causes that agitate the air from month to month. We need to resist the reduction of imaginative truths to a succession of historicities that lead to an unending fashionable up-to-dateness. As a resister I harp on the permanences and the continuities of the humanistic substance; but as a theorist of duality, I point also to the temporal aspect of humanistic experience: we do take the humanities as contemporary, we do read them with a new eye different from that of the 1870s, and we do pay some attention to new things which may turn out to be wholly transitory.

We can further understand what our comic mode is by seeing clearly what it is not. For instance we always speak loosely of the inner relationship between comedy and tragedy, as if at a touch one form might undergo transubstantiation into the other. Perhaps, in some ways, this is so. But there is one irreconcilable difference: the disparateness which in comedy we accept and live with is the truth that in tragedy tears us apart. In tragedy we do not compromise or serve several gods; we must assert one imperative over another, or our own mad will over an imperative, and so we prepare our ruin. In tragedy, duality means irreparable dividedness; in comedy, the endurable complications of actuality. Comedy can be almost as sharply distinguished from punitive melodrama and black comedy. Here we come back again to the two ultimate counterattitudes to the world that we have been mentioning but mainly holding in reserve until they could help illustrate educational comedy. I refer to an unrestrained hatred of the world and an uncritical love of it, or, in our special terms, an underacceptance and an overacceptance of it. The acceptance of disparateness falls squarely between these extremes of hate and love, or, in other terms, nausea and lust. One noncomic extreme wants to enforce a single standard of life, the other doesn't dream that there is more than one way of living. One wants to transform, punish, or destroy the world, and these processes are not always distinguishable. The other side rejoices in the world as it is: it scrambles up the ladder, hops aboard, makes hay while the sun shines, gets a finger in the berry pie, etc.

With its tolerance of duality, education feels great pressure from both single-minded extremes—the pressure of exhortation and accusation. Neither side wants education to accept the disparate, that is, the other. Hence we receive wonderfully inconsistent accusations from the world. For the first three decades of my academic life we were accused of siding with those who would wholly transform life, would conserve nothing, would radically reorganize the world. In my fourth decade the greatest volume of sound has come from those who accuse us of being only worldlings, servicing the world, holding it together, concealing its obsolescence. The very inconsistency of these outcries suggests that we have persisted, however imperfectly, in our comic acceptance of not altogether congruous realities. Each complainant wants to use education in a single role, to turn it into a melodrama of good guys against bad guys, whether the good guys are the total transformers or the total maintainers. No one in search of power likes the middle-ground position that looks in both directions at once; one side wants education to be all defense, the other side all attack, whereas it has to be something of both. To coerce education into total partisanship, one faction attributes all evil to the system and the establishment; it ignores the fact that there will always be a system and an establishment, always conducted by men and women of the same human imperfections. If we recognize this fact and remember to accept the disparate, we escape the disastrous folly of going new left or dead right.

We have to accept man as both knower and mover. The pressures from both sides want to make him only a mover: the ruin of the high comic enterprise of education. Moving begs the question of ends, and it is hostile to knowing, which might question ends. Our problem, however, is less with anti-intellectualism in the world, which I am convinced is an overrated danger, than with antifactualism in humanity. The acceptance of facts to which we are committed sounds easier than it is, for people work hard at denying facts. Take the fact of mortality: we make monstrous efforts to deny it. Hence our fantastic—and I begin to think questionable—expenditures for medical research. If the billions spent on cancer and heart research since 1920 had gone into other projects, there would by now have been many an indignant call for public investigation. Not here, for we crazily dream of a world without terminal illness. (This has to be said by someone who on an actuarial basis is somewhat closer to termination than many others.) Again a great deal of millennial thought seems to deny the fact of human perversity, whether it takes the form of envy, malice, or destructiveness; we forget disparateness in imagining mankind naturally equipped for whatever ideal we aspire to. We tend to feel that unpleasant facts can be coerced out of existence by resolute action, in either legislatures or streets. Some good academics that I have seen campaigning against war seem to take no account at all of man's native disposition to war and warlike conduct, though they reveal the disposition daily. Prospero is nicer than Caliban, but is he more frequent? In one frame of mind we forget the epigram of Eddie Carbone in Miller's *View from the Bridge*: "Most people ain't people." In the opposite frame of mind we also forget that man is capable of generosity and sacrifice: it is easier to settle for the mechanical half-truth that if man seems selfless it is only because he is suicidal.

I've been trying to make concrete the ways of rejecting a disparateness which in education we have to accept. In our internal professional practice this acceptance means, among other things, that field specialists abstain from promotionalism and profit-seeking for their own fields. It means that in the humanities we keep aware of the precarious balance between the scientific and the intuitive, and aware that if we accept only one, at the expense of the other, we become trivial. When a praiseworthy concern for the demonstrable gets out of hand, we shy away from important subjects. The opposite danger is perhaps a more serious one, for our field happens to attract individuals of great self-absorption, who easily feel that letting fly with their own subjectivities is an inherently valuable mode of professional activity. On the one hand, the individual imagination must vivify the texts that we present; on the other, some people believe that what they "want to do" in offering and designing courses takes precedence over all the claims of the material that needs to be taught.

As accepters of the disparate we acknowledge the merits of doing one's thing, but we also ask, Is it worth doing? and, Is the doing worth anything? Or we may say, Do your thing, but don't do it to me—or others. Again, in response to the clamors against delivering information in the classroom: we of course admit that information may be a substitute for thought, but we likewise insist that without information there is no thought at all. In another direction, accepting the disparate means keeping our scholarly games in balance with workaday classroom business. I'm not against games; I just want us to identify many of our specialized activities as games, so that we will not speak of them with the tedious solemnity often created by the single standard of values. The acceptance of disparateness means, to drop to lower-drawer business, that the dissertation director will not assume that the choice of him by a Ph.D. candidate indicates only the superiority of the candidate. But after many years of observing dissertation directors I suspect that in this area the acceptance of disparateness has hard going.

Finally the acceptance of disparateness means keeping a sharp eye on the doctrine of relevance, one of the more seductive of the siren voices luring us from comic wholeness into a single-viewed melodrama. A few relevancy people are pure schemers: they want either to do away with education as a bar to their own ends, or to make it a tool of their own ends—punishing the world, transforming it, or possessing it.

168

Hence their call for relevance is a slogan to deceive, or a war cry to galvanize, the numerous innocent followers needed to create an air of popular pressure. To repeat, in education we must see man as both changing and unchanging, as attached to the timeless as well as the timely. The relevance cliché, as it is popularly accepted, would simply cut out half of this dual sense of man, and, in the humanities, the more indispensable half—the sense of the complex nontemporal nature of man against which all causes have to be measured. If we stick to that, we are true to our own nature, and, in a more practical way, we protect the innocent relevancers against themselves, against the sad misconception that there is a special education for 1973 and that we must produce it. If we did somehow whip up such a contrivance, think of what and where the victim of it would be as early as 1977, when the educational blueprint for 1973 would be dated. Imagine the utter confusion in the year 2000, with the world populated by the incompatible alumni of a series of outmoded relevant educations of which no one can remember the once persuasive rationale. No student can know what will be relevant for him in a decade; few can even know what is really relevant at the time being. If we can protect the innocent relevancers against themselves, we will help protect a future in which they and others will all have a share. Maybe we can understand relevancers better if we think of them as the modern counterpart of the tradeschool boys who once seemed the chief threat to humanistic education.

I recently heard a member of a distinguished English department commenting on the fact that the department had dropped Old English as a Ph.D. requirement. He said, "We soon found we had made a mistake. The humanistic tradition is indivisible. But we divided it, and we then learned that we had opened up an endless nibbling away at it." We might say that the department had gone for a fashion, and that fashions are the overt symptoms of creeping relevance. Since we do accept the timely—a phase of the disparateness of the world—we will not totally avoid fashions. There are fashions in courses, and we all know the current ones: interdisciplinary, literature through films, literature through linguistics, violence in literature, minority subjects, and anything that can be called innovation. There are fashions in dissertation subjects, as I know from reading many applications. Some years back the grotesque had quite a run for several seasons. Then existentialism ran rampant through the carrels, and absurdity and selfcreation were being discovered everywhere. The early 1970s thing was phenomenological criticism (perhaps, as a modernist colleague alleges, an oxygen mask for existentialism). Then came the landslide topic of literature of, by, and for women. Some of this is inevitable. What we can at least do is see whether we are maintaining disparate claims or are being dominated by the chic, that is, the single value that excludes all others. Relevance may mean, too, the ad hoc remedy that sees only one fact. A few years ago a shortage of Ph.D.'s led to the new insight that the producers were too few and the years of study too many; by multiplying one, and decreasing the other, we soon turned out an oversupply of Ph.D.'s. Will we now discover that the producers are too numerous, and the training years too few?

We need not make too much of any single phenomenon of adjustment. What is worrisome is the sum total of pressures to get with the world in its regular changes, to make education transform wholly, or adjust wholly to, the world. It is too easy to lose the sense of disparateness and to fall in with the world as it is, as it is becoming, or as it is envisaged in some new state free of human dross, and to lose our sense of the persistently human from which we may derive some critical detachment. Two excellent dramas of our day show how seductive is a world-in-becoming, even to academic characters. Both are dramas of disaster; in both we see professorial types in the grip of a single limited perspective, the putsch of the times. In Max Frisch's *Firebugs* a couple of modern destructive types, disguising themselves in a deficiency of privilege and of justice, methodically destroy a civilization by burning down one house after another. We professors appear in the character simply known as "the Ph.D." Up to the end he is all on the side of the arsonists because, as he says, "I was intent on improving the world." He has lost sight of any other role. Only too late does he find out that improving the world is not what the arsonists were up to. Then he issues a formal statement dissociating himself from the final big burn when all goes up in smoke. Ionesco's *Rhinoceros* shows a community first startled and outraged by a rhinoceros that crashes destructively through the town; then the community is gradually transformed by a creeping movement in which, after initial resistance and then with all kinds of justifications, virtually everybody joins up and becomes a rhinoceros. Academe is represented by the character simply called the Logician: he insists, as rhinocerism grows, that the only problem is to find the correct way of defining the problem. In my present terms, he accepts only one pole of reality: the theoretical approach, here in its taxonomic aspect. He seems very detached and secure, but he has nothing substantial to balance against the fashionable downward thrust, and we soon see him running with the rhinoceroses. What Ionesco very subtly conveys is that totally joining a new-world movement is much like totally joining the world as it is—in either case a single-valued act which discards the obligatory acceptance of disparateness.

Frisch and Ionesco give very vivid pictures of educators going completely relevant and thus failing in their true role.

In Congreve's *Way of the World* Mirabell and Millamant do not flee
from the world. They do not flog it. They do not free it or frame it
anew. They accept it for certain comforts and customs that it affords.
What they do not do is accept it totally. They erect a code of personal
conduct which is more exacting than the code of the world. They use
no sonorous or self-adulatory terms, but what they seek is an enduring
dignity that will not succumb to fashions, even though they live in a
world of fashion. They never think of themselves as exemplars, nor
could they conceive of themselves as enforcers. But in maintaining a
tension between the personal and the worldly, they do afford a model
which, just by its presence, might help preserve the world against its
own built-in tendency to drift downward. Even through a veil of
difference we can imagine them as a model for institutions like ours
that function by combining an acceptance of things with a sense of
unacceptable things.

Seventy-five years after *The Way of the World* Sheridan's *School
for Scandal* reveals in comedy a declining acceptance of disparateness. It
begins to repudiate the world; it sets up an alternative standard of the
good heart. Fortunately it does not altogether succeed because Sheridan's wit and imagination keep parting company with his act of will
and his formal intention. Yet he moves definitely toward sentimentality, toward the condition of much of the drama of his day and of
many following days, in which the comic acceptance of the disparate
gives way to a melodramatic sense of the irreconcilability between the
good guys and the bad guys. Is it more than a coincidence that the
universities of Sheridan's day were at a low level of respectability?
Perhaps, if they moved in a way parallel with comedy, they lost a
maintenance of different values held in fructifying tension, and fell too
far into worldliness or unworldliness. The penchant for the single
standard shows in one aspect of a slightly earlier scholarship: the adjustment of Shakespeare and Chaucer and ballads to Augustan taste.

In comedy the butts are the single-trackers—those who become
solemn, self-righteous, indignant, censorious, or punitive, who reject
the disparateness of the world but want the world to adopt their single
track. Two traditional single-trackers are the fops and the rustics (*The
Way of the World*, by the way, shrewdly presents the underlying link-
age between these opposites). In the comedy of academe these contrasted types are the intellectual dandies and the intellectual boors—
those in whom thought is replaced by an excessive refinement of taste,
one form of single-standardism; and those who are mechanical, obtru-
sive, heavy-handed, implicitly rude to the intellectual community,

the single-standardism of men who accept the inner push and coarse dogma but not the way of the world that would tone them down. In their opposite ways both fail in the grace of mind that the humanities, if we believe our own words, tend to establish in man. Another graceless character, also a butt in comedy, is the neurotic, not so much the innocent sufferer as the man who makes his disorder a plague or punishment to everyone else. One version of this has been nicely called "paranoia for power," or, alternatively, the world as therapist for oneself, or vice versa. In the humanities we find apparently unwell characters, or perhaps just misguided ones, who would use our materials for therapy of themselves or of the world, or for sorcery, to cast devils out of the world—that is, it often appears, to eliminate the unlike rather than accept the disparate. We survive, however, if these types do not become so numerous as to reduce or eliminate two other experiences associated with comedy—the laughter and the partially happy ending. In a world that at times seems humorless we can but hope that we shall not have to substitute tears for laughter, as in eighteenth-century sentimental comedy. As for the happy ending: it is that sort of accommodation in which everyone, so to speak, gets something he hadn't had before, perhaps not all he would like, but, if he is lucky, a Mirabell-Millamant standard as a private directive, and takes it into a world which he neither flees nor conquers but accepts in its duality. He even accepts, if he finds it so, the fact that he and the world are not at one. The one type incapable of this happy ending is the unyielding rejector of the disparate—that is, the fanatic, the doctrinaire, the scourge, the man who knows that his heart is the repository of the good, the single good, good for all, compulsory for all.

In trying out the notion that higher education, and especially our brand of it, is in the comic mode, I am of course playing a game of analogy or metaphor—funambulistic, I admit, but I hope not ruinously so. Such a game is not philosophically defining. If it works right, it may be a little stimulating or evocative. Naturally good comedy is not programmatic, so that I can hand down no decalogue of essentials for the humanities. Still, to think of a serious business as comedy-like may have an advantage or two. It may sneak in a lighter tone in a rather somber age (I may, alas, have fallen into a little somberness myself, at times). It may guard us against solemnity about our role, especially in a day when some propose for the humanities a religious function. The humanities are not the center of a religion, and the comic sense may protect us against becoming sonorous priests of sacred books—sacred books which, when they fall into the hands of Puritan schismatics, may be viewed as giving literal guidance in secular affairs. If the notion of our style as comic should at all stir the imagination,

this stirring might, in time, subtly influence choices of actual procedures in humanistic education. Out of that schooling should come, at
least, an awareness of the diverse modes of human functioning—
modes that appear in the mind, and on the stage, and in society. The
awareness should be not only of what the different generic modes are,
but also of where each is fitting and of why they should not be confused or interchanged. One will know much if he knows when to be
melodramatic or tragic or comic, and how to be. As humanistic educator he will be at his best if he masters that open sensibility of comedy
which manifests itself in the acceptance of disparateness. This acceptance may mean bearing with the contradictory and the inconsistent, or
with the tendency of now to become then and vice versa, or with the
tendency of good and evil to be kissing cousins. Or it may mean an
unwillingness to settle exclusively for either half of the various dualities inherent in human life—for the actual or the dreamable, for the
active or the contemplative, for the immediate and changing or the
nontemporal and the permanent.

To comprehend both is to espouse a complex middle truth against
two matching simplistic excesses—overadjustment to the world and
overrefinement, on the one hand, and, on the other, underadjustment
to the world and barbarism. What the two extremes have in common,
despite all their differences, is self-absorption, assertive egotism. Overadjustment uses the way of the world for self-interest; overrefinement
is the self-serving attenuation of civilized norms. Excess profits and
excess in culture are related forms of egotism, of Luciferian pride. At
the other extreme, underadjustment pits the raw self and crude dogma
against the way of the world, and insolently denies the authority of
civilized norms. It is only a step to the barbarism that destroys. This is
the coarse Luciferism of envy. These versions of egotism, since they
would render the social world uninhabitable, are the ultimate serious
butt of comedy—on the stage, and in academe.

Special Acknowledgments

The author and the publisher are indebted to the following journals and organizations for permission to reprint these essays: to the Association of Departments of English for "The Ghost on the Ramparts," *Bulletin of the Association of Departments of English*, no. 19 (October 1968), 3–12; to the National Council of Teachers of English for "Except He Come to Composition" and "The Full Man and the Fullness Thereof," *College Composition and Communication*, XXI (October 1970), 230–44; "The Cult of Personality," *College English*, XXIII (November 1961), 91–98; "Teaching Careers and Graduate Schools," *College English*, XXXII (April 1971), 754–59; and "Literature and Growing Up," *English Journal*, XLV (September 1956), 303–13; to the University of the South for "The Antiquarians and the Up-to-Date," *Sewanee Review*, LX (Summer 1952), 522–25, "Historian and Critic," *Sewanee Review*, LXXIII (Summer 1965), 426–44, and "Critics, Clichés, Anticlichés" (original title of "Clichés and Anticlichés"), *Sewanee Review*, LXXVI (Winter 1968), 145–58; to the *Southern Review* for "Humanistic Education as Comedy," *Southern Review*, n.s., VIII (Summer 1972), 548–71; to the *Texas Quarterly* for "Outside the Laws," *Texas Quarterly*, V (Spring 1962), 33–42; to the *Western Humanities Review* for "Fashions in Melodrama" (original title of "Humanisticism and Melodrama"), *Western Humanities Review*, XIII (Winter 1959), 3–15, and "Freedom from Speech," *Western Humanities Review*, XV (Spring 1961), 99–110. "Verbal Traffic and Moral Freight" appears in print for the first time.

Index

175